1966

THE GOOD, THE BAD AND THE FOOTBALL

Bruce Talbot and Paul Weaver

SUTTON PUBLISHING

First published in 2006 by
Sutton Publishing Limited · Phoenix Mill
Thrupp · Stroud · Gloucestershire · GL5 2BU

British Library Cataloguing in Publication Data
A catalogue record for this book is available from the British Library.

ISBN 0-7509-4029-8

To our Mums

Page iv: Batman on the cover of *Life*, 11 March 1966. *(Yale Joel/Life
Magazine/Time & Life Pictures/Getty Images)*
Page vi: Twiggy and Justin de Villeneuve. *(Ted West/Central Press/Getty Images)*

Typeset in 10.5/14 pt Sabon.
Typesetting and origination by
Sutton Publishing Limited.
Printed and bound in England by
J.H. Haynes & Co. Ltd, Sparkford.

CONTENTS

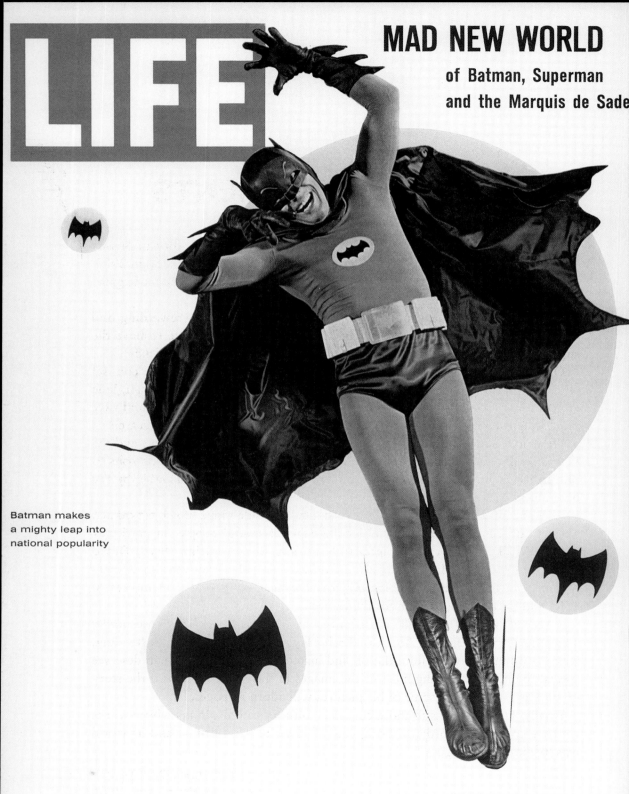

LIFE

MAD NEW WORLD

of Batman, Superman
and the Marquis de Sade

Batman makes
a mighty leap into
national popularity

MARCH 11 · 1966 · 35¢

ACKNOWLEDGEMENTS

Our first book, *The Longest Journey*, pieced together the story of Sussex County Cricket Club's historic first County Championship success in 2003. For two Sussex followers who earn their living writing about the summer game it was very much a labour of love.

This project was much more challenging, but it has been a rewarding and enjoyable one nonetheless and once again we have been fortunate to have the support and assistance of so many individuals as well as family and friends.

Our agent, David Luxton, offered abundant enthusiasm and wise counsel while, at Sutton Publishing, Sarah Bryce, Christopher Feeney, Jane Entrican, Jane Hutchings and Glad Stockdale made sure the project got off the ground and gave unflagging encouragement and advice throughout our long months of research.

We would like to thank our respective employers, the *Brighton Argus* and the *Guardian*, for their forbearance and use of their extensive archives. Our visits to the British Newspaper Library at Colindale were made more enjoyable by the helpfulness of their diligent and friendly staff.

As you can imagine with a book covering such a wide range of subject matter, we have drawn upon the personal recollections of several people. In particular we would like to express our gratitude to Rob Boddie, Brian Ward, David Miller, Jim Mossop, Mark Anderson, John Sullivan, Mike Donovan, Ian Aitken, Natalie Craig and Kevin McNamara for sharing their personal memories of 1966 and for their enthusiasm for the project.

A special word of gratitude must go to Sheila Lewis, for talking so candidly about her bereavement at Aberfan. Trish Hayes, at BBC Archives in Reading, was a constant source of information and inspiration. James Boardman deserves special thanks for sourcing most of the images in the book. Perhaps if the story of 2006 is ever written, some of his pictures will adorn its pages.

Finally, sincere thanks to those countless authors and historians whose works we have consulted in order to bring you a flavour of what Britain and its world was like forty years ago.

Bruce Talbot and Paul Weaver
Brighton, April 2006

INTRODUCTION

It is uncertain when the Sixties started and finished. Historians squabble when asked to decide, precisely, when the Palaeolithic became the Mesolithic and then the Neolithic period in Stone Age Europe, and it is much the same here.

One day, perhaps, archaeologists will come up with the definitive answer, but it is not a calendar thing. Students of politics, fashion and music would all produce different answers. Beatles fans, for example, would say that the Sixties started with the release of the Fab Four's first album, *Please Please Me*, in 1963, and ended with their last, *Abbey Road*, in 1969. Those with an interest in politics might argue that the opening years of the decade, when the prime minister was Harold 'You've never had it so good' Macmillan and then Alec Douglas Home, were more truly representative of the Fifties, and that the Sixties were ushered in when the younger Harold Wilson, with his 'white heat of technology' speeches, became PM in 1964.

There is a sense that the Sixties – that is, the essence of the time – started much later than some suppose, and kept going longer than others would have it, into the early Seventies, perhaps. What is beyond question, is that 1966, whose 40th birthday we celebrate this year, was both chronologically and culturally bang in the middle of the Sixties, the most exciting or the most decadent decade of the last century, according to your point of view, and certainly the most iconic and exciting period that many of us have lived through.

This was the year that *Time* magazine declared London to be a 'swinging city', when you were no one unless you strutted Chelsea's King's Road. Carnaby Street was fashionable and so were the haircuts of Vidal Sasoon. Mary Quant appeared on the Queen's birthday honours list – just as The Beatles had the year before. England won the World Cup for the only time to date, and were beaten by the cricketers from the West Indies . . . not for the only time.

There was the general election that would finally allow Harold Wilson's Labour Party to stamp its authority on the period; or not. And there was the tragedy of Aberfan, which concentrated the grief of these islands on a small mining village in south Wales. But even more relevant than what happened in 1966 is the fact that the year was at the eye of the cultural and sociological storm.

Sex, we were told, was invented in 1963. There was the Pill, which was a landmark breakthrough because it liberated women – though some women argue that it did the opposite and merely put more pressure on them to have sex. There was also fresh legislation relating to abortion, divorce and homosexuality. This was when the young challenged the old. They always have, of course, but now there was a fresh vigour in the polemic. It was the beginning of the end of the age of deference, which was certainly a good thing, but also, as a consequence, the beginning of the end of innocence, which is often the source of much regret.

It was the decade of comprehensive schools and pirate radio stations, of mods and rockers and pop art. There was the Great Train Robbery and the hunt for Ronnie Biggs. There was also the hunt for the spy George Blake, who escaped from Wormwood Scrubs using a ladder of knitting needles.

President John Kennedy was assassinated in Dallas in 1963 – and yes, it's true, most of us can remember the date, 22 November, and what we were doing at the time. He had had to handle the Cuban missile crisis, which many thought would plunge everyone into a third world war.

But there was a war in Vietnam. And there were the assassinations of Martin Luther King and Bobby Kennedy, which both happened in 1968, the same year Louis Armstrong sang 'What a Wonderful World'. Britain's most famous wartime leader, Winston Churchill, died a more peaceful death in January 1965.

There would be rivers of blood, Enoch Powell told us. Well, there were riots in Notting Hill and the National Front did seize the imagination of a disagreeable minority. It was the time of the miniskirt and the Mini, not to mention the small-wheeled Moulton bicycle. The growth in motorways and personal wealth led to a boom in motoring. Ford launched the Cortina in 1963 and followed it with the Escort (1968) and the Capri (1969). For others, with no kids to worry about, the Jaguar E-type was the car to be seen in. Certainly its daring design made contemporaries such as the Sunbeam Alpine and the Austin Healey Sprite look pretty ordinary. It was the time of Woodstock and drugs, of *Coronation Street*, supermarkets and colour telly. The trade

Double agent George Blake absconded from prison using a ladder made of knitting needles. *(Copyright © popperfoto.com)*

union movement began to rumble, ominously, and John Profumo, the Conservative cabinet minister, got himself into an awful tangle with a showgirl named Christine Keeler.

There was less religion and more spiritualism – certainly church-going declined in 1967 when many preferred to stay at home and watch *The Forsyte Saga*. There was a huge jump in consumerism and advertising. It was the beginning of the buy now, pay later generation as HP agreements and then credit cards took off, ushering in a new kind of poverty.

Some people were so greedy they even started buying dishwashers, for goodness sake. And wall-to-wall carpets, courtesy of Cyril Lord, became quite the thing. There was a surge in DIY, both in the home and in the garden. And the kids were kept amused munching a wide variety of new sweets that had come on the market, including Twix and Marathon (1967), Topic (1962) and Toffee Crisp (1963). But After Eight mints (1962) and Matchmakers (1968) were put on the top shelf for adult use, only if these adults weren't lighting up one of the wide new range of tipped cigarettes, for filter brands represented healthy smoking at the time. Children, meanwhile, sucked on sweet cigarettes, fostering a dangerous habit.

Magazines such as *House and Garden* shaped our tastes and there was a gradual move away from the purely utilitarian towards the luxury end of the market, increasingly reflected in the advertising of the time.

We started eating Heinz Spaghetti Hoops (1966), Smash instant potato (1968) and Mr Kipling's Cakes (1967). And the mess could be cleared up using the J Cloth (1967). And there was Britain's very first fabric softener, Comfort (1967), followed by Ariel (1969).

There was a drive to make housing available for all. But terrible decisions were made in the world of architecture as high-rise buildings went up while historic town centres were swept away. The damage to civic pride in many large communities was significant.

If there were difficulties on this planet there was great interest in others as America and Russia embarked on the space race, which may have been a branch of their Cold War activities but was great fun for everybody else.

That led, in 1961, to Major Yuri Gagarin becoming the first man in space. And it would be followed, eight years later, by America's Neil Armstrong walking on the moon, with one of the century's most famous quotations: 'One small step for man, one giant leap for mankind.'

There are strident voices, and they tend to come from the right of the political spectrum, who declare that this was the decade when we were delivered to the gates of hell. They throw their arms up in horror at the hedonism and decadence of it all.

An article in the *Daily Telegraph*, by Anthony Lejeune, on 12 April 1966, summed up the misgivings of many:

Anyone who has travelled abroad during the past few years, or who talks to foreigners visiting Britain, must be aware that there are, to put it mildly, aspects of the contemporary British scene which have not merely surprised the outside world but which increasingly provoke its contempt and derision.

One of the first things which strikes anybody is the physical appearance of many young people: the extraordinary long hair of the boys, the unkemptness of the girls, the weirdness of the clothes.

London has been described as the fashion centre of the world – which would once have meant that the tailoring is unmatched in its quality, durability and classic good taste – where the most extreme of juvenile fashions originate and proliferate. Britain also has the dubious international distinction of being hailed as the Mecca of pop music.

It cannot be wholly a coincidence that the new swinging London is also a city in which crime and drug taking have increased alarmingly, though Britain's juvenile delinquents may still seem innocuous compared with the dangerous young animals who prowl the streets of some foreign cities.

He concluded that the breaking down of discipline, of traditional structures and of established values were 'symptoms present during Rome's decline'. Get the gist? The likes of Mr Lejeune still exist and some would even have us believe that the decade was a myth, that somehow we had made a jump from the years of continued rationing and post-war austerity in the Fifties straight into the grimly disappointing Seventies. For them the Sixties never really happened. Or, if it did, it was some awful aberration before the resumption of normal service. In truth, though, nothing would be the same again.

For this was the time when the Establishment rocked on its foundations, when the old order was fiercely questioned, as if by Radio 4's John Humphrys, and would never again exert quite the same authority. Forelock-tugging ended here.

It did not lead to revolution because the British, unlike the French, are not a revolutionary people. Downing Street was not torched and the decline in the popularity of the royal family was still many years away.

But this was still the age of a new liberality. There were the hippies and drug-taking became a major issue. The sensational rock musical *Hair* represented the abolition of stage censorship.

And what about literature? At the start of the period it was still illegal to publish D.H. Lawrence's *Lady Chatterley's Lover*. But by the end of it we were reading Philip Roth's *Portnoy's Complaint*.

Private Eye, edited by Richard Ingrams, was launched in 1961. And from Australia there came the brilliantly illustrated *Oz*.

The *Daily Herald* was replaced by the *Sun*, then a broadsheet, in 1964, long before Rupert Murdoch bought it and transformed it into a brash and hugely popular tabloid in 1969. The *Daily Mirror* and the *News of the World* were the most successful popular papers of the time.

And right in the middle of this dysfunctional and sybaritic family of years, his long hair divided only by the glow of a shared party splif which allows us to glimpse his ennui, sits the proud figure of 1966.

This is not a history of that year. We have not ransacked *Hansard*. We have not investigated the unemployment or inflation figures or pored over the minutes of various planning subcommittees or even engaged in meaningful dialogue with sociologists. Nor have we been enslaved by a sense of chronology. If anyone can discern a sense of order here, he or she is much cleverer than us.

What we have done is attempt to capture the essence of the year. The World Cup was its greatest joy, Aberfan its sorest wound.

Politics, even if you prefer to ignore the subject and pretend that all the parties are the same anyway, is always profoundly relevant to our lives and this was most certainly the case in the Sixties.

Music and fashion were the tools of self-expression then, as they are now. Television had replaced radio as the main source of home entertainment. Films, whether they were viewed in the cinema or on TV, continued to be immensely popular, whether they dealt in fantasy or the need to explore the world in which we lived.

All these subjects are looked at here as we attempt to recapture – by snapshot rather than long reel – a year that was quintessential Sixties, perhaps the most remarkable decade of the century.

It was not a great year for everyone, certainly not for the creator of Donald Duck and Mickey Mouse, Walt Disney, nor for the novelists C.S. Forester and Evelyn Waugh, nor Buster Keaton, perhaps the greatest of all stars of the silent screen; they all died.

Many of us had not been born then. One of your authors was just an infant; the other was 14, and looked at all the extraordinary goings-on as a boy might stare longingly into the windows of a closed sweet shop. We have taken the precaution of speaking to more reliable witnesses.

1

HOW THE WORLD WAS WON

England's victory in the World Cup was quite the most memorable thing that happened in 1966. That is not to say that a mere football match was more important than the tragedy that befell Aberfan, or even the result of a general election that would shape the political landscape for the second half of the decade.

But Aberfan, though embedded in the minds of all those who read and watched the reports, with their moving monochrome images, is somehow not instantly associated with the year in which it occurred. There was no umbilical link to 1966. Many people think that it happened years earlier and it feels as though it truly belongs to the first half of the twentieth century, if not the previous century.

As for Harold Wilson, well, he won four general elections out of five and is perhaps better remembered for coming to power for the first time in 1964. But everyone knows which year England won the World Cup; many could pick the month and some even the date.

This was the World Cup, held in England for the first time, which saw North Korea confound the pundits by beating Italy and go 3–0 up against Portugal. It was the World Cup of Pelé, Eusebio and Yashin. But, even more memorably, it was the World Cup of Moore, Banks, Charlton and Hurst.

The sense of achievement shimmers still, bright even among the most treasured of memories. On Saturday 30 July 1966 England beat West Germany 4–2 and lifted the Jules Rimet trophy.

Every four or ten years an anniversary is held, the old heroes are herded together once more and the vivid colours are refracted through time's prism. Actually, it happens more often than that. For as Gary Lineker once observed, with unconscious humour, 'The World Cup is every four years, so it's a perennial thing.'

So spectacular, so clear is the recollection that it tends to overshadow the fact that England's footballers had won nothing worthwhile before that date – and have not done so since. Yet it colours our expectations, as it has always done, for the 2006 tournament.

Today, when even the result of a dull play-off final in one of the lower divisions can lead to bacchanalian behaviour and the most hedonistic of drunken excesses, it is worth remembering that the overwhelming urge for many people, when it was all over on that wonderful Saturday afternoon in 1966, was to put the kettle on and make a nice cup of tea. The heart may have been pounding but the spirit of John Mills was alive and well in households throughout the land. In joy, as in despair, the stiff upper lip served well. Yes, of course, some drink was taken. But it was all a little restrained by modern standards.

In Euro '96, again staged in England, the level of expectation was overwhelming. And Terry Venables and Paul Gascoigne made so much noise that you would have been forgiven for thinking that they had won the thing.

In 1966, the excitement took a while to catch on. Rob Boddie, 59, a Brentford supporter, said:

> The whole thing didn't really take off until we played Argentina in the quarter-finals and we realised we had a chance of winning the World Cup. It was a sudden awareness, for most people, that we really could go all the way.
>
> The Argentinians were kicking everyone in sight. Alf Ramsey called them animals. And he had Rattin in mind in particular. After that match I went down to the ticket office and they asked me how many tickets I wanted for the semi-final against Portugal. It would be unheard of today.
>
> I didn't decide to go to the final until the morning of the match. When I mentioned it to my dad he gave me a fiver, though I didn't need that much.
>
> I walked down Wembley Way, as casual as you like, and gave a ticket tout fifty bob for a 25-shilling ticket. There were plenty of them about. I bought one for my late wife, Lynette, though she didn't like football much.
>
> And afterwards, well, I had a few beers. But no-one went mad. The idea wasn't to get drunk in those days. A few thousand of us went to the Royal Garden Hotel in Kensington, where the team had a reception. But it wasn't anything like Liverpool after they had beaten AC Milan in the Champions League last year.

The full-house crowd paid a record £204,895 in gate receipts. The Royal Garden Hotel had opened only a few months earlier. Mark Anderson, the hotel's Director of Sales and Marketing, said:

> Up until a few years ago there were a number of people still working here who remembered that famous day. The last one who was involved left a year ago. But everyone working here now still knows about that World Cup win

and the part the hotel played in the celebrations. And guests who know their history will occasionally comment on it.

We are planning a special dinner for July 2006, and have spoken to the Bobby Moore Foundation about raising money for cancer research. The hotel, which is much the same from the outside as it was then, has been famous for its sporting associations ever since, with various football teams staying here and, from the world of rugby, the All Blacks and the Wallabies. Last summer the Australian cricket team were based here when they were in London.

In the days, weeks and months following the World Cup, the man who scored the first hat-trick in the final got so fed up with being asked: 'Are you Geoff Hurst?' that he would often reply: 'No, I'm not. My name is Brian Ward,' a name he made up. The real Brian Ward admits he has never been mistaken for Geoff Hurst, but he was one of the thousands who watched England's moment of triumph.

It's not hard to imagine the sort of hysterical reaction there would be in England if David Beckham brings the World Cup back from Germany this summer. How different things were forty years ago. There was no waiting list for tickets, no-one applying had their credentials questioned, you didn't have to be a member of the England Travel Club and there wasn't even any segregation in the crowd for either the group matches or the final, when England and West Germany supporters stood side by side on the terraces exchanging banter and bonhomie. Brian Ward now lives in retirement in East Grinstead with his wife Shirley, whom he met in 1966, and these days watches his football at his local club in the Sussex County League. He recalls:

We were able to buy a block of tickets for all the games at Wembley pretty easily. They were the six Group One matches, a quarter-final, semi-final and of course the final. It worked out perfectly of course. We saw the three group matches, the quarter-final against Argentina and then the semi when Bobby Charlton scored those two wonderful goals against Portugal.

I'll never forget the day itself – well you wouldn't forget something like that, would you? Memories fade with time of course, but that was simply unforgettable. Myself and some mates from work stood behind the goal where Geoff Hurst scored the second goal of his hat-trick – the one which caused so much controversy.

Of course we couldn't tell from where we were whether it had crossed the line or not, but I will always remember the reaction of Roger Hunt. A forward's instinct when the ball is on the line is to tap it in and claim the goal but Roger just raised his arms and started celebrating with Geoff.

When the final whistle went we just started hugging complete strangers. It was one of those experiences I think only football fans can relate to. But I don't remember people crying tears of joy or anything like that, there were no wild shows of emotion. We were all a bit reserved in those days.

But all the way back to central London the crowds were singing and celebrating – which you expected.

However, by the time I got off the train at Merstham everything had calmed down. I was going to see Shirley and walking along the streets you wouldn't have thought sporting history had been made a few hours earlier. You couldn't hear any parties going on or anything like that. Most people I spoke to afterwards watched it on TV, enjoyed the moment, put the kettle on and then got on with the rest of their Saturday night, you know – mowing the lawn or something like that.

As for the man himself, Sir Geoff Hurst is probably more revered now than he was those forty years ago when the most famous hat-trick in the history of football secured England's triumph.

Hurst could scarcely have imagined then that four decades later football fans, many of whom weren't even born in 1966, would happily pay good money to hear him reminisce about his career, which brought 24 goals in 49 appearances for his country, and in particular that memorable day at Wembley.

And why shouldn't he cash in on his celebrity? Winning the World Cup itself didn't make him rich. The twenty-two-man squad were each given a £1,000 bonus by the FA but his match fee for each game was a modest £60. And he sold much of his memorabilia a few years ago, including his red shirt, to provide for the future financial security of his family.

In the past fifteen years the after-dinner speaker circuit has become a growth industry of its own. Hurst restricts himself to two or three such engagements a month but he remains a huge draw. Of his contemporaries, only Jimmy Greaves – the man whose place in the final he effectively took – and Alan Ball are in as much demand as Sir Geoff who, at 64, looks just the same as he did at his moment of triumph.

Of course, the waist has thickened slightly since his playing days and the hair is a little thinner, but he is fit and trim and puts that down to regular visits to the gym near his Cheltenham home.

His playing career, particularly at his first club, West Ham United, was legendary. In 502 games he scored 252 goals before moving to Stoke where he made 128 appearances and scored 37 goals. After a season with West Bromwich Albion and a brief period with non-league Telford he retired and joined his old West Ham boss Ron Greenwood as part of the England coaching set-up between 1977 and 1982.

Not so well known, perhaps, were his two largely unsuccessful years as manager of Chelsea, which ended in 1984 when he left football to move into the insurance business.

He remained largely out of the public eye for the next decade or so, but the surge in the game's popularity – and in particular that of the England team – during the Nineties has catapulted Hurst and the other members of the most famous England line-up of all time back, reluctantly in some cases, into the spotlight again.

At sporting dinners these days he is treated with almost reverential respect. Guests queue up patiently to get their old programmes and England shirts autographed between courses while others happily fork out £30 for a grainy print of 'that' goal adorned with a flourish of his thick black pen with the number '66' after every signature. Nice touch, that.

Mind you, Sir Geoff is well aware of his own commercial value. He hates the thought that his name is being exploited, that he is being ripped off. He won't sign certain items for fear that they will end up being sold on through internet auction sites.

He has a nice line in self-deprecating humour, too. Once the applause has died down after he is introduced to the audience (and if there is anyone in British sport who doesn't need an introduction it is surely him) he opens with the line: 'Thanks very much, I'm glad you remembered me.' Now instead of applause there is gentle laughter.

For the next half-hour or so he will have the punters eating out of his hand as he recounts those golden days of Greavesy, Bally, Mooro and, of course, Sir Alf. There are one or two withering barbs about some of the players who have worn the Number 9 jersey for England since him, but the crowd don't want to hear his views on Emile Heskey. The story of how England won the World Cup has been recounted a thousand times, but to hear it from the man himself? Well, that's what it's all about isn't it?

The speech is over and his disciples form another orderly queue in front of the top table. Hurst is unfailingly polite and happy to talk. For him, at least, the enjoyment of that high summer's day in 1966 will last forever.

The memories came flooding back to Nobby Stiles in 2002, as he watched another World Cup from his hospital bed while recovering from a heart attack. In his autobiography published the following year, which is one of the better examples of the genre for it was ghosted by James Lawton and titled *Nobby Stiles After The Ball*, he said:

I thought of all the tension and the worry before that final explosion of joy and relief which sent me jigging across Wembley. I saw the banners again and I heard the cheers.

I remembered how calm Bobby Moore had always been, and the time when Bally was left out of the games against Mexico and France and after collecting some winnings from the bookmaker's, throwing the fivers on the floor and dancing on them, saying, 'Fuck Alf Ramsey,' but I knew that really he was breaking up inside because you only had to look at his face to know that.

I couldn't forget the look on the face of Jimmy Greaves, one of the greatest players English football has ever seen, when he began to realise that the tide of good fortune was, for him, maybe ebbing away.

I thought of the surge of electricity that shot through the team and Wembley and, I'm told, the whole nation when Bobby Charlton scored his stupendous goal against Mexico – the one that told us that we really were in with a chance of winning the greatest prize in all of football.

Most of all, I recalled the brilliant leadership of Alf Ramsey and the loyalty he showed to me when I was being hung, drawn and quartered by the press, the television panellists and the high-ups in the Football Association, and the world ruling body FIFA wanted me thrown out of the tournament following a tackle.

The memories, of course, are strong with all the surviving players, including goalkeeper Banks. Banks, though, is also a little peeved about how little he and the rest of the team earned from their famous victory. In his autobiography, *Banksy*, published in 2002, he said:

Nobody plays in the World Cup just for the money. And just as well, too, in our case. We received a bonus of £22,000 from the FA which, to the unanimous agreement of the players, was divided equally among the squad.

That gave us all £1,000, taxed at 40 per cent in those days, so we received £600 each for winning the World Cup. By contrast, an enterprising street vendor, who posed as a press photographer, screen-printed some T-shirts and sold them outside Wembley before our games. He told us he made over £1,500.

The late Kenneth Wolstenholme, the commentator who famously said 'Some people are on the pitch, they think it's all over – it is now!' had the good sense to copyright those words. Ken told me that over the years he made more money from the royalties than the entire team earned for winning the World Cup.

That tale sounds particularly poignant following Alan Ball's decision in 2005 to sell his winner's medal in order to raise money for his family. Not that any shortage of wealth inhibited the players when it came to celebrating.

Football writer James Mossop remembers how the players let their hair down after the game: 'It might have started quietly but after they won it the celebrations were big.' And Mossop knows because he took part in them with Jack Charlton.

> I was working in Manchester at the time but I came to London for the match and being a keen young reporter I went to the team hotel when it was all over thinking I might pick up a story.
>
> There, I bumped into Jack Charlton. All the wives were there apart from Jack's because she was expecting a baby that weekend. I knew him from way back and he said, 'Come on, we're having a night out.'
>
> I told him that I only had a tenner but he took £100 out of his top pocket and said he had been given it by Adidas for wearing their boots in the final. 'We'll spend this and yours too,' he said.
>
> Harold Wilson was leaving the hotel at the time so we ducked behind his car, which you couldn't really imagine happening today, and jumped into a taxi. It was only then that we realised there was somebody already in the taxi. He didn't know that England had just won the World Cup. He was a classical musician who had just played in a concert in the Wigmore Hall!

Charlton and Mossop had a few drinks at a West End club called the Astor and were then approached by a complete stranger, Lenny, who invited them to his table for more drinks. They spent the night sleeping on Lenny's London sofa.

When Jack had a walk in the garden the following morning a woman popped her head over the fence and said, 'Hello, Jackie!' It was a neighbour from his home village of Ashington in Northumberland who was visiting relatives in London.

'When we went back to the hotel the following morning Jack had a message tied round his neck saying "Please return this body to room 606",' Mossop recalls. 'His mother was waiting for him and gave him a ticking off for being out all night. It brought a World Cup winner down to earth!'

The elder of the Charlton brothers may have been returned to terra firma but, four decades on, many of us remain in orbit with the mere memory of those wonderful deeds, played out on a sunlit afternoon in north London. Time and again the match, or at least the goals and thrilling climax, is played to us again, even though many of us have it tucked away somewhere on a dusty video cassette.

The players, some looking a little grisly now, are trotted out for dinners or charity functions, their anecdotes so deeply ingrained on the memory that they might almost be the cast of Agatha Christie's *The Mousetrap*, London's longest-running play.

We won the Cup. Jack Charlton gives Alan Ball a lift as the nation celebrates with a nice cup of tea. *(Copyright © popperfoto.com)*

We all know what they are going to say, even the inflections of the voice. We know when the jokes are coming. But they are never boring because they gave us the greatest moment of our own sporting memories. We simply love them all for that. And if you don't, you just don't understand.

THE MANAGER

Sir Alf Ramsey, England's greatest football manager, originally wanted to be a grocer. Born in Dagenham in 1920, his life was transformed when he joined the Duke of Cornwall's Light Infantry in 1940.

Playing for his battalion against Southampton, he was on the wrong end of a 10–0 defeat but so impressed the club that they signed him on amateur forms. Ramsey was a forward in those days but when he turned professional in 1944 the Southampton manager, Bill Dodgin Senior, decided to play him at right-back. Four years later he won his first England cap against Switzerland at Highbury. The following year, in 1949, he moved to Tottenham, where he made his name as an integral member of Arthur Rowe's 'push-and-run' side, along with Eddie Bailey and Ronnie Burgess.

Ramsey, nicknamed 'the general', remained at right-back where he played behind the future great Spurs manager Bill Nicholson at right-half. But he often foraged forward and became famous for the accuracy of his free kicks.

His lack of natural pace left him vulnerable to the left-winger who attacked him – and Billy Liddell and Bobby Mitchell did. But his awareness and tactical skill placed him ahead of other, faster players – perhaps this was why he admired Bobby Moore so much.

Spurs won the second and first division titles in successive seasons, 1950 and 1951. He became manager of Ipswich, then in the third division, in 1955. In his second season, with the famous strike partnership of Ray Crawford and Ted Phillips, Ipswich were promoted to the second division. In 1961 they won that division and in 1962 they finished top of the first division.

When he was asked how he felt about that he replied: 'I felt like jumping over the moon.' A cliché was born. It was at this time, Brian Glanville suggests in his very readable *Football Memories*, that Ramsey first thought of taking elocution lessons. 'He once told a restaurant-car steward, in very affectedly posh tones: "No thank you, I don't want no dinner."'

Ramsey was appointed England manager and with uncharacteristic bravado he announced that England would win the World Cup in 1966. His reign, though, did not start well. In his first match, against France in Paris in the Nations Cup, early in 1963, England were beaten 5–2.

He won the World Cup with a 4–3–3 (or 4–4–2) formation, a team that became known as the 'wingless wonders'. But until then he had been in favour of wing play, always stressing the importance of getting round the back of a packed defence. On a chilly December evening in 1965, in the Bernabeu Stadium in Madrid, Ramsey played Alan Ball, Nobby Stiles and Bobby Charlton in midfield, with George Eastham, Joe Baker and Roger Hunt up front. They won 2–0 and Ramsey said later: 'It was after the Spain game that I realised England could win the World Cup with this system.'

His most controversial decision, however, was to dispense with Jimmy Greaves, the greatest English inside-forward and goalscorer of his or perhaps any other day. Greaves was a great player, though one strangely allergic to World Cups.

He had disappointed in 1962 and now injury and indifferent form ensured that he would do so again and Ramsey, as the tournament progressed, hardened towards a strike partnership of Roger Hunt and Geoff Hurst.

Greaves, though, had not made a good start with Ramsey. In May 1964, a little more than a year after taking the job, the manager took his England team to Lisbon for an international against Portugal.

On the eve of flying out the team gathered at the Lancaster Gate Hotel. Ramsey imposed a curfew but seven players – Greaves, Moore, Eastham, Banks, Johnny Byrne, Ray Wilson and Bobby Charlton – headed for the West End. Greaves said later: 'There were not many footballers who could match Mooro in a drinking contest.'

They went to a bar called The Beachcomber and Greaves added: 'It was odds on the night would become something of a stagger before it was through. We got stuck into a drink called a Zombie – rum-based with a real kick.'

According to Banks it was 1 a.m. when they got back to the team hotel. They thought they had got away with it but when they reached their rooms they found that Ramsey had placed their passports on their beds.

After a training session in Lisbon he said: 'I think there are seven gentlemen who would like to stay behind and see me.' Then he told them: 'If I had enough players here with me, none of you would be playing in this match. Just learn a lesson that I will not tolerate the sort of thing that happened in London before we left. We are here to do a job for England and so am I. Thank you gentlemen and don't let it happen again.'

Two weeks later, though, Greaves and Moore, great friends, went on another binge during a trip to America and Moore almost lost his place in the side to Norman Hunter of Leeds United. It was only just before the World Cup that he and Ramsey were properly reconciled.

It never happened for Greaves, though. Many felt that the Spurs player was desperately unlucky, and they were right. But others made the point that the majority of his goals at international level had come against weaker opposition. Bobby Charlton appeared to support Ramsey, albeit retrospectively, when he said a few years later: 'Jimmy was a bit of a luxury, in all honesty. I always felt he would score five if you won 8–0, but in matches where a single goal would decide it was better to have someone like Hurst. You never saw Jimmy much in a game. He was waiting there to score and I suppose that's why he never materialised for Alf.'

The players – most of them, anyway – respected Ramsey's authority. They also played for him because he was intensely loyal. The best example of this came in the victory over France. Late in the game, Stiles committed a particularly nasty foul on Jacky Simon in front of the Royal Box. Two Football Association officials ordered Ramsey to withdraw Stiles from the team for the rest of the tournament. Ramsey reminded them that he was in charge of team affairs and that if Stiles went so would he.

Jack Charlton was once asked by a friend what Ramsey was like. 'I don't know,' he replied. 'I was only with him six years.'

In his autobiography Charlton continued:

Alf was a very difficult man to get close to. He spoke a bit like a schoolmaster, with the clipped tones of a man who had once taken elocution lessons. He was not the sort of manager you could sit down with over a couple of beers at the bar to discuss things, like you could with Don Revie.

Alf was a stickler for time. With Don, if you were playing a hand of cards or watching a movie the night before a game he would let you finish before going to bed. Not so with Alf. Alf would come in and announce, 'Bed! Time to go' – and you had to go. One night he packed us off while we were watching *Butch Cassidy and the Sundance Kid*, so that we never saw the end. I'm still trying to find out if they got away! I was once standing having a quiet drink at the bar when Alf came in and said, 'We're still on the pints, then, are we Jack?'

I didn't know how to react. I've never been a big drinker and I was just having a quiet pint before going to bed. Maybe he didn't mean anything by it – or maybe he did. I never thought he liked me, to be honest. But I learned a lot from him.

Ramsey was always worried about his players' fondness for a pint or four. After the semi-final win he told them: 'Gentlemen, congratulations on a fine performance and on making the final. You have done well for yourselves, for me and, most important of all, for your country. But tonight, I want you to have just two pints. After the Argentina game you were, well, how can I put it, rat-arsed. But not tonight gentlemen. Just two pints because we have a World Cup to win on Saturday. When you do it, I will make sure that you are then, and for quite some time, permanently pissed.'

In Mexico in 1970 England were, arguably, an even stronger team and, with Moore looking even more commanding than he had done four years before, they had a wonderful chance of reaching at least the final.

But Banks fell ill after a dodgy glass of beer and his replacement, Peter Bonetti, was not quite up to it on the day. England lost to West Germany in León after leading 2–0. It was the first World Cup in which substitutes were allowed and Ramsey didn't play them cleverly. He took off Bobby Charlton, who was bossing the game, in order to rest him for the next match, the semi-final, and England surrendered control. Bobby Charlton never played for England again.

It was the beginning of the end for Ramsey, though it was another four years before he was forced out of office. 'Most managers, at any level, have a finite usefulness,' said Brian Glanville. 'And Ramsey was no exception. By 1972 he was not the same man. It became quite clear when England met West Germany at Wembley in the quarter-final first leg of the European Championship that year. To my amazement, he had picked a team without a single tackler in midfield. In consequence, the big-booted, long-haired Gunter Netzer ran riot and England lost 3–1.'

Ramsey returned, briefly, to club management with Birmingham City, but with little success and he retired to his beloved Ipswich where he died in 1999. He was not impoverished but nor was he a wealthy man. And he never had the personality to make the most of TV punditry, even if he had wanted to. Not everyone agreed with his methods. Even some years after the World Cup was won Malcolm Allison, one of the most colourful of football personalities, particularly when he was managing Manchester City, said: 'Sir Alf's elevation of power beyond skill was his most consistent contribution to our national team. We won the World Cup with a good side which had some very ordinary players and we are still suffering.'

There is much in that, even though Allison's legacy is not a lasting one. British football, however, has always had a fundamental physicality at its core. Alf Ramsey still pieced together the team that would bring England the greatest moment in its rich sporting history. And, forty years on, we still forgive him his methods. Stiles has certainly 'forgiven' him. At the final whistle, back in 1966, he said to his manager 'You did it, Alf! We'd have been nothing without you!' And he was right.

THE PLAYERS

The essence of the England team, for all the great talent possessed by Banks, Moore and Bobby Charlton, was hard running and a strong team ethic. They were mentally and physically strong and thoroughly well prepared by Ramsey. There were few individuals capable of stopping you breathing with a moment of wonder. Its real strength was organisation and a burning desire.

In goal, Banks had established himself as England's finest since Frank Swift. He had made his debut at home to Brazil in May 1963. Brian Glanville said of him: 'A Sheffield man who played for Leicester, he combined physical strength and courage with astounding agility. His high cheekbones, his narrow eyes, gave his face an almost Red Indian, rather than a Yorkshire, look. He was modest, quiet and diligent.'

Even now it is difficult to think of a better goalkeeper in an England shirt than Banks, whose save against Pelé in the 1970 tournament is still replayed to this day as one of the miracles of the game. He was massively good and his confidence spread out towards the defenders in front of him.

Ray Wilson, a veteran of the 1962 campaign, would play right-back and the other full-back would be Fulham's George Cohen. Jack Charlton said: 'In George and Ray we had two really quick attacking full-backs. George in particular used to tear up and down the field. We used to laugh at George, because he was a bloody awful crosser of the ball. I mean, he would run three-quarters of the length of the field with the ball – and then cross it behind the goal. We used to shout, "George, just keep it in play!"'

Wilson did not come forward as often as Cohen but, when he did, he did so with real speed and intent. And in the middle of the defence was Jack himself, not gifted like his brother but full of experience and aggression and blossoming at Elland Road under the management of Revie. With his height he was also a threat in the opposition's penalty area.

Beside him would be the inspirational Moore, not the quickest but a great reader of the game, a wonderful tackler and as comfortable on the ball and as good at passing it as any midfielder. He transmitted his calm authority to the whole team. 'Bobby never had any pace,' said Jack Charlton. 'In sprint training he was always the last. But he was such a good reader of the game that he would often be already in position and able to anticipate an opponent's pass.'

Hurst said: 'They said he couldn't run, but he was rarely beaten to the ball. They said he couldn't jump, but he was rarely beaten in the air. He recognised that he was deficient in some areas and compensated by working hard on the training pitch and focusing on his positional play.'

In midfield there was Bobby Charlton to run things. He was perhaps the finest midfield player produced by England. He was not a dribbler, a tricky ball player like his contemporaries George Best and Charlie Cooke, but dropped shoulders, body feints and outstanding acceleration saw him drift past opponents.

A converted left-winger, Ramsey brought him into the centre. He had out-standing vision and passing ability. And he was a terrific, two-footed goalscorer.

Stiles remembered almost coming to blows with another Manchester United player, Paddy Crerand, about the latter's assertion that Eric Cantona was a more important player than the younger Charlton. 'Bobby had natural power and wonderful balance, exploding off either foot, and the first time you saw him play you knew you would never forget that initial impact on your imagination. "Doesn't his World Cup goal against Mexico count – the one that made us believe we could win the greatest trophy in football?" I spluttered to Paddy. "Or the one in the European Cup final against Benfica? Or the two that beat Portugal in the semi-final of the World Cup? Or all the forty-nine he scored for England, which twenty years after he stopped playing remains the all-time record? Or the 253 he scored for United?"' As TV viewers of the time would readily testify, Crerand rarely made any sense in arguments.

Then there was the little redhead with the squeaky voice. Alan Ball was just 21 but full of passion and running and a great one-touch player. He had been turned down by Bolton as a boy because he was too small. 'You'd make a good little jockey,' they told him. He was still playing for Blackpool but would have an outstanding club career with Everton and Arsenal on his way to becoming one of England's most capped players. One day, according to Stiles, Ramsey went up to Ball and asked: 'Do you have a dog at home?'

Ball said he did and Ramsey was ready with a follow-up question. 'Do you take it for a walk, and if you do, do you have a bone with you – or a ball?'

'I take a ball,' said the little maestro.

'What do you do with the ball?'

'Well, boss, I throw it for the dog.'

'What does the dog do?'

'He goes and gets the ball and brings it back to me.'

'Exactly,' said Ramsey with a tone of triumph in his voice. 'That's what I want you to do for Bobby Charlton.' Ball knew exactly what his role in the team was. But what a pedigree dog he was.

Beside him was Stiles, less creative but stronger in the tackle. Tiny, toothless and almost hairless, he looked as if he should have been queuing up at the post office to draw his pension. There was no great pace or passing ability but he was a great competitor and the sort of man-to-man marker that forwards have restless nights about. He would play the great Eusebio out of the game in the match against Portugal and his euphoric, gummy jig after the final victory over West Germany would become one of the great symbols of the occasion.

In another life he would rejoin his Manchester United colleague Bobby Charlton at Preston, but they had had their glories.

Then there was Martin Peters, a player famously described by Ron Greenwood as being ten years ahead of his time. He was a West Ham player, like Moore and Hurst, but one whose abilities were more difficult to define.

Unpredictable, but skilful and aware, he had the ability to turn up in the penalty box at just the right time. 'Martin ghosted around the pitch creating space not only for others, but for himself,' said Banks. 'He impressed me with his great sense of positioning and vision, the more so since he was only 22 years of age.'

The defence and the midfield looked strong. But the attack, without Greaves, was hardly designed to frighten the world's best defenders.

Roger Hunt was a prolific goalscorer for Liverpool. Strong and determined, he always worked hard. But he was not the stuff of a centre-back's nightmares. Nor was Geoff Hurst, though he would become the only man to score a hat-trick in a World Cup final. This former Essex Second XI cricketer was once a wing-half and an ordinary one. But, tall and strong, he always had the physique of a centre-forward and here he thrived, taking blows unselfishly and running off the ball.

Individually, then, it was not a great team. Portugal and Hungary might argue that they were more skilful sides in that tournament. And England did not even play well until they had reached the semi-final. But when it mattered, England played better than anyone else in the world.

It is a sad feature of this team that so few of them went on to achieve success in the game in later life. Only Ball and Jack Charlton went on to manage at the top level and Ball, mostly, was a dismal failure.

The saddest case of all was Moore, who would die of cancer in 1993, aged 51 – he had been diagnosed with testicular cancer as early as 1962, the year his England career took off, but it was hushed up.

His various businesses, like his dabbles in management, ended in failure, but it was surprising that the Football Association never found employment for its only World Cup winning captain. He ended his professional life as a commentator for London's Capital Radio, and his colleague and friend Jonathan Pearce told the *Observer* recently: 'This huge effect Bobby had on people – whether it was for thirty seconds or thirty years – to have lost that in life is tragic enough. But for the game never to have employed that and to never have benefited from that is a scandal. An absolute scandal. Why was he never used in an educational role? Or a figurehead role? Or a [Trevor] Brooking role? What a waste.'

ENGLAND'S EARLY MATCHES

Before England won the World Cup they lost it. In March 1966, the 12in tall, 9lb trophy was on display as part of a stamp exhibition in Central Hall, Westminster. It disappeared while a Methodist service was being held in the rest of the hall. The theft was first noticed by security guards at 11 o'clock. A door in the exhibition room had been forced and a small padlock at the back of the glass cabinet had been removed. But the stamps, which had a sporting theme and were valued at £3 million, had not been touched. English football's collective red face was saved a week later when it was discovered in some bushes by a dog called Pickles. Pickles is the forgotten hero of the 1966 World Cup.

As for the football, England had won all three games on a warm-up tour of Europe and went into the tournament with some confidence. But it started miserably, with not a whisper of the glory to come. England's first match, at Wembley, was a sterile affair against a grimly unambitious Uruguay side. Everyone said that Greaves should have played in the final against West Germany but he made little impression in the opening fixture, though neither did his rival Hunt. And Bobby Charlton, his old enigmatic self, gave no clue of what was to come.

In his autobiography, Jack Charlton said: 'Uruguay had some very good, gifted players, and it surprised me that they didn't come for a result. They came for a draw and the game finished 0–0. Jimmy missed a couple of really good chances, they had just one shot over the bar, but that was that. It was a very disappointing start for England.'

Their next match was against a Mexico side that also packed its defence. They succeeded in frustrating England and their supporters until, seven minutes before half-time, Bobby Charlton scored one of the goals of the tournament, gliding past two players before shooting powerfully from 30 yards. Jack recalls: 'Our Robert scored one of the best goals ever seen at Wembley. He picked up the ball in our half of the field, turned, and started to run with it. The Mexicans backed off him a bit, then he dipped his shoulder and went past one of them. I was right behind him, and I wanted him to shoot, but he didn't. He went past another guy – and then he struck the ball with his right foot, about 10 yards outside the 18-yard box. It just flew, it was a goal from the moment he struck it. Tremendous goal.'

Hunt scored the second in the 2–0 win but it was hardly inspirational stuff. It didn't get any better in the final group match against France, although the game was again won 2–0. The most memorable thing to happen in the match was that foul by Stiles on Simon.

It was, though, a watershed. Afterwards, Ramsey laid into his players. But the team that would ultimately reach the final was finally beginning to take shape. This was the last game in the tournament that Ramsey deployed a conventional winger, Ian Callaghan of Liverpool. An injury to Greaves concentrated the manager's attention on Hurst and the absence of Ball made everyone's heart grow fonder.

THE OTHER GROUPS

For the second World Cup the planet's biggest star, Pelé, was laid low by injury. Had he managed to avoid the flaying boots of his opponents, Brazil would surely have at least reached the knockout stages. As it was, the abiding memory of Pelé's World Cup was the sumptuous free-kick with which he scored in their 2–0 win over Bulgaria at Goodison Park in their opening fixture. It was to be their only victory in Group Three.

Brazil were back at Everton to face Hungary in the pouring rain a few days later. This match, many observers argued, was the game of the tournament and, in the absence of the injured Pelé, it was dominated by Hungarian midfielder Albert who had the English crowd chanting his name in adulation by the end. Hungary won 3–1 as their attackers picked regular holes in a ponderous Brazilian defence. It was the holders' first defeat in the finals since 1954, but it was to get worse.

Having to win their final game against Portugal to reach the knockout stages, Brazil made seven changes and brought back Pelé, even though he wasn't fully fit. One of the new faces was goalkeeper Manga. Nicknamed Frankenstein, he crossed himself nervously in the tunnel before kick-off.

When it came to crosses on the pitch he was pretty hopeless, punching Eusebio's early centre straight to Simoes, who made it 1–0. Eusebio quickly scored a second, following good work by the powerful centre-forward Torres.

With the match under control, there seemed little need for Morais to end Pelé's tournament with a cynical foul. Amazingly, he stayed on the pitch but the ten men were given hope when defender Rildo scored in the second half. But Eusebio made it 3–1 following a corner and Brazil were out.

Portugal had opened their campaign with a 3–1 win over Hungary at Old Trafford and both teams subsequently defeated Bulgaria to qualify for the quarter-finals. The shock result of the group stages – and one of the biggest upsets in World Cup history – took place at Ayresome Park, where North Korea defeated Italy 1–0 in their final match in Group Four.

The Koreans had started badly. Russia bullied them in their opening game and won 3–0, but there was evidence of the speed and agility of their players in their next match against a poor Chile team, which ended in a goalless draw. 'The Koreans played with splendid spirit and refreshing sportsmanship,' according to Glanville in his definitive *History of the World Cup*. 'The kind of professional foul to which the World Cup exposed them clearly filled these straightforward little men with pained surprise.' But they could play a bit too and began to sense a nervousness in Italian ranks. They scored the only goal of the game in the 42nd minute when Pak Doo Ik rifled a shot past goalkeeper Albertosi. Incredibly, they had qualified for the last eight along with Russia who had won all three games. Chile finished bottom, having collected just a point from their draw against North Korea.

Italy headed home in shame, but the embarrassment continued for their players for many months afterwards. Mocking chants of 'Ko-r-ea' would ring out around Italian grounds whenever any of the World Cup side were in action.

In contrast to England, West Germany's progress to the last eight was relatively serene. They opened at Hillsborough against Switzerland with a 5–0 stroll, Franz Beckenbauer scoring twice in his first appearance in the finals. The Swiss had dropped two of their best players for breaking a curfew and paid the price. There was early evidence of sharp practice by the Argentinians against Spain at Villa Park where Spanish playmaker Suarez was on the receiving end of two hefty challenges early on. In a poor match, Argentina won 2–1 and then drew 0–0 in Birmingham against the Germans despite having Albrecht sent off in the second half for a foul on Haller. Uwe Seeler, who had only just recovered from an operation to fit an artificial Achilles tendon, scored the winner in the 84th minute as Germany secured their place in the quarter-finals with a 2–1 win over Spain.

Argentina also went through after defeating Switzerland 2–0, but England supporters had been made aware of the threat the South Americans would pose in the last eight. England's group offered few thrills for what neutrals there were.

Uruguay booked their place in the quarter-finals with a scoreless draw against Mexico in their last match, having defeated France in their opening fixture 2–1. London boasted some fine football stadia at the time but the match was actually played at White City in the west of the capital.

THE QUARTER-FINALS

England had reached the quarter-finals. And there they played Argentina in the nastiest game of the tournament. Much better than that was the game between Portugal and North Korea.

Bobby Charlton said afterwards: 'I quickly discovered that whenever I beat an Argentinian I could expect to be tripped, body-checked, spat at or dragged to the ground.'

Glanville recalls: 'The Wembley match, or fiasco, would reverberate for years to come, would polarise European and South American football, evoking almost paranoiac reactions from the River Plate.

'The Brazilians were already away, arriving by train at Euston with the faces of condemned men, muttering, not without justice, of the inadequacies of English referees. Now Argentinian cynicism and provocation met the authoritarianism of Herr Kreitlein; and all was chaos.'

It was after this game, Leo McKinstry reminded us in his fine book, *Jack and Bobby: A Story of Brothers in Conflict*, that the system of yellow and red cards came into being. 'It was the English official, Ken Aston, who came up with the idea when, driving away from Wembley at the end of the quarter-final, he was stopped at a set of traffic lights.'

It didn't help that miniature Kreitlein spoke neither English nor Spanish. Argentina embarked on a spoiling game from the starting whistle. Antonio Rattin was booked for a foul on Bobby Charlton which was by no means his worst.

Nine minutes before half-time Rattin, the Argentina captain, was sent off, but refused to go. He strolled around insulting various members of the crowd and anyone else who came his way before finally being persuaded to let the others get on with the game. It was won by Hurst, playing his first match of the finals, in the 77th minute. Peters sent over the near-post cross from the left and Hurst met it with a glancing header.

Tempers frayed, too, at Hillsborough were West Germany eventually overwhelmed a Uruguay team who finished with nine players 4–0. Haller's first-half goal gave the Germans an advantage they scarcely deserved, for Uruguay had opened brightly. The turning point came when the South Americans claimed a shot had been handled on the German line. Emmerich lashed out at Uruguay's captain, Troche, who responded by kicking him in the stomach. He was sent off and slapped Seeler's face for good measure on his way back to the dressing room.

The South Americans accused Germany of play-acting. At one point Haller collapsed to the ground, writhing in agony. An opponent had grabbed him by the testicles and later that night Haller discharged blood.

When Haller was scythed down by Silva, Uruguay were down to nine men. They clung on until twenty minutes from time when Beckenbauer, revelling in the extra space, made it 2–0. Further goals from Seeler and Haller put the Germans into the semi-finals. Hungary had been the outstanding team in the group stages. Now they disintegrated against a powerful Russian side at Roker Park. Another Hungarian goalkeeping error, this time by Gelei, allowed Chislenko to score an early goal and when Gelei failed to collect a corner, shortly after half-time, Porkujan poached a second to put Russia in command. Hungary pulled one back through Bene and Lev Yashin produced a wonderful save in the dying stages to preserve Russia's lead and secure their semi-final against the Germans.

THE SEMI-FINALS

For the first time England showed what they could do. In Portugal, they were up against one of the best footballing sides in the tournament and England were allowed to play football themselves.

Bobby Charlton had scored before in this tournament but now he really imposed himself on the entire game. He also rolled in England's first goal after Peters had sent through Hunt, whose shot was blocked.

After that England missed a number of chances. And they seemed likely to pay for their profligacy in the opening fifteen minutes of the second half which were dominated by Portugal's skilful forwards. But Moore, Jack Charlton, Banks and Stiles defied everything thrown at them.

England regained their fragile ascendancy and, eleven minutes before the end, scored again. Hurst used his strength to resist a challenge and pulled the ball back for Bobby Charlton to score. It was just getting comfortable when Portugal pulled one back. Jack Charlton, who for once had met his match in the air in the powerful Torres, was penalised for hand ball and Eusebio scored from the spot. This inspired Portugal to a final flurry of attacking moves in which Stiles, leading the resistance, was magnificent. He was England's man of the match – after Bobby Charlton.

Banks said: 'The match belongs to Bobby Charlton more than anybody. He gave the greatest performance of his life.' There was even a call for a statue of the player to replace that of Lord Nelson in Trafalgar Square.

The final beckoned. But not for the great Eusebio, who left Wembley in tears knowing that now he would never be a World Cup winner.

In contrast to the thrills at Wembley, the other semi-final, played a day earlier at Goodison Park, was dreadful. Glanville called it a 'sour, ill-tempered, impoverished match refereed without illumination by the handsome, obtrusive Sicilian Concetto Lo Bello'.

Two minutes before half-time Chislenko, Russia's hero against Hungary, was sent off for recklessly kicking out at Held, having only just hobbled back onto the pitch after receiving treatment following a heavy tackle. Haller gave West Germany the lead and Beckenbauer scored a second from a free-kick in the second half. Porkujan pulled one back late on, but Russia were out.

THE FINAL

You may have heard about what happened here, at Wembley, on 30 July. Germany won. No, only kidding. The images of the game, and of the celebrations that followed, are so familiar now that it easy to forget the fierce debate that preceded the match: should Greaves play?

He was fit again, having been injured in the game against France. He had scored forty-three goals in his fifty-four games for England. But he hadn't done much in the opening three games of the finals, just as he had disappointed in 1962.

Predictably, Ramsey, faithful to his players and his instincts, continued to have faith in Hurst.

In sixty-five years West Germany had never beaten England. They had only managed one draw in all that time. Ray Wilson said: 'After playing Portugal in that super match in the semi-final, we were quite relaxed about the final in the end. I don't want to discredit them but they had never beaten us at that time.'

This time, largely neutralised by the magnificent Franz Beckenbauer, Bobby Charlton did not exert such a powerful influence. And there big worries when Germany took the lead when Wilson, uncharacteristically, headed Held's left-wing cross straight to Haller, who brought it down and scored. Six minutes later, England were level. Moore took a quick free kick on the left and delivered it onto the head of Hurst, who nodded home.

After that the match could have gone either way. England's pre-match confidence looked a little misplaced as Germany, led by Seeler and Held and with Beckenbauer pushing up to midfield, looked a different side from that which had overcome a dour Russia in the other semi-final.

Even now, watching that final over again, you sometimes feel that Germany really were the better team, that on this umpteenth showing they just might go on and win. With only twelve minutes remaining, Peters put England 2–1 ahead.

There was less than a minute to go when Jack Charlton, perhaps unluckily, was judged to have fouled and from the free-kick Wolfgang Weber scored; 2–2. There would be extra time for the first time since Rome in 1934. Banks recalls:

It looked a harsh decision to me and Jack wasn't happy about it either. In his view the foul should have been given the other way for backing in. Lothar Emmerich drove the free-kick into my penalty box, which was a sea of red and white shirts.

I thought I saw Schnellinger help the ball on with his hand. The ball bounced across the face of my goal towards the post with me in hot pursuit. Wolfgang Weber came sliding in. I saw that Ray Wilson had extended a leg to block the ball should it come low, so I threw myself with my arms outstretched above Ray's leg. One of us was bound to block Weber's effort.

Wolfgang Weber was a highly intelligent footballer. He was quick off the mark but his mind was even quicker. He assessed the situation immediately and lifted the ball with the toe of his boot. Ray tackled fresh air, I grasped at nothing and the ball shot over both of us and into the net.

I felt as if the bottom had dropped out of my world. Glory had been snatched away. In a matter of moments I felt deep disappointment, anger, self-pity and, finally, determination. We hadn't lost.

Moore later revealed how Ramsey dealt with extra time. 'Alf was un-believably good. He could have come on screaming and shouting, hollering and hooting, saying "I thought you'd know better. I thought you'd have learned after all those years as professionals." Instead he said: "All right. You've won the World Cup once. Now go and win it again. Look at the Germans. They're flat out. Lying down on the grass. Having massages. They can't live with you. Not for another half-hour. Not through extra time."'

England looked flat out themselves. But that certainly didn't apply to Ball, who was an inspiration in that last half-hour. Hurst scored again via the underside of the crossbar, with perhaps the most controversial goal in history.

The goal was only given after a lengthy consultation with the linesman. TV replays would never prove, beyond doubt, that the ball had crossed the line. But if it hadn't why did Hunt, who was nearby, raise his arms in celebration rather than provide the finishing touch? The debate goes on, and will do for ever.

There was no doubt about England's fourth, a net-bulging score by Hurst. Stiles and Cohen embraced each other like long lost lovers; Bobby Charlton sank to his knees; Ball did a cartwheel; Banks punched the air; Jack Charlton looked heavenwards and wept; Hunt also looked up, with outstretched arms.

Jack Charlton still marvels at the pass by Moore that set up Hurst for his hat-trick goal.

The second half of extra time seemed to last for ever. Then came Bobby Moore's bit of magic. It was typical Bob. He was under pressure in the box when he took the ball on his chest and pulled it down.

Was it over the line? Roger Hunt is certainly convinced as Geoff Hurst's shot comes back off the underside of the crossbar. *(Central Press/Getty Images)*

I couldn't believe it when he passed to Bally, who passed it back again. I mean, you just don't do that when you're defending in your own box – especially not in the last minute of a World Cup final! I humped any ball that came my way as far as I could, into the crowd, anything.

You don't try to play yourself out of trouble. Which is what Bob did, and then he stopped and turned and looked upfield before delivering the perfect pass for Geoff to run on and score the fourth goal. I didn't actually see the goal, because I was looking at Bob and thinking 'I will never be able to play this bloody game' because Bob has just done something that is unheard of.

That Moore pass is often passed over in favour of other fabulous moments. But Banks, like the elder Charlton, will cherish it for ever. 'Bobby's limbs must have been terribly weary, but you'd never have known it from the way he played that ball downfield. To this day I find it hard to believe that, so late in the game, Bobby could emerge from defence with such élan and retain the necessary vision to execute such a deft pass over such a distance.'

England had won the World Cup. And a nation was uplifted. This was, and is, the very essence of sport. Experiments have been done with cats in which they have been woken up whenever they have started to dream; they died. So would we. And just as dreaming is essential to human life (we do it whether we think we do or not) so there is the need to dream in our waking hours, too.

Sport, perhaps more than any other escapism, allows us to suspend belief. It lends us vicarious delights. And it's no good people saying it's only sport because sport, by its very nature, has an importance out of all proportion to other matters for the dedicated fan. Some heartless souls would have us believe that sport belongs to life's toy department. But it is more than that. And this was the greatest moment in the long, sweaty, muddy, muscle-wrenching history of British sport. The ecstasy of the players was shared by millions more.

The last word must go to the patrician Geoffrey Green of *The Times*, then the doyen of football writers. In his book, *Great Moments in Sport: Soccer*, he recalled:

> For days, weeks, maybe months afterwards they [the players] were kicking themselves.
>
> So, too, were others of us, the sceptics, who from the start thought the feat beyond our reach. But it was no dream. England, as a side, perhaps did not possess the same sensitive flair of Hungary or Portugal that summer.

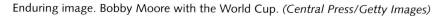

Enduring image. Bobby Moore with the World Cup. (*Central Press/Getty Images*)

Hungary, indeed, had they possessed a class goalkeeper, might well have been the final victors.

But in the last analysis Bobby Moore and his men were the best prepared in the field, with the best temperament based on a functional plan. Also they had a fine defence and, further to that, they built to a peak. The timing of it all was good.

And never had Wembley itself provided a more emotional setting. From early afternoon the atmosphere fairly crackled. The terracing was a sea of waving flags, the standards of two nations; the noise was a wall of sound that drowned the flutterings of one's heart. High in the stands there came the beating of a drum, a deep, pulsating thud which was almost tribal.

It set the mood of a throbbing match, climaxed in the sunshine of the end when the Germans, honourable losers, made their own farewell lap of the stadium to a warm reception and followed amid thunderous roars as the stadium rose to Moore holding the golden, winged trophy in triumphal circuit. Honour and justice was done in that proud moment beyond many dreams.

Well, OK, not everyone was as reserved and stiff upper-lipped as John Mills.

2

REVOLVER AND OTHER PET SOUNDS

At Christmas 1966, when Tom Jones seemed to be in permanent residency at the top of the charts with 'The Green, Green Grass of Home' – the year's biggest selling single – and artists like Val Doonican and The Seekers were challenging him for the year's most coveted number one spot, you could have been forgiven for thinking that in the middle of the most celebrated decade in the history of popular culture, the British music scene had become ever so slightly sugar-coated. Even the *Sound of Music* soundtrack had been the best-selling album for nearly eight months of the year.

American artists, in particular The Beach Boys and Bob Dylan, were beginning to exert more of an influence on the British charts – and the thinking of British musicians – than at any time in the decade thus far. But this was still a golden era for British music even though it was a time when people thought Lulu was a rocker and The Tremeloes were wild.

Historians still regard 1966 as the year the long-playing album was truly invented – and we're not just talking about Cliff Richard's *Kinda Latin*. *Revolver*, *Aftermath*, *Pet Sounds* and *Blonde on Blonde* were all released and sold by the truckload in this year.

Yet a lot of the most popular groups of the time, such as The Small Faces, The Kinks and The Who, were still ostensibly regarded as singles' artists. But put *It's All or Nothing*, *Dead End Street* and *Substitute* on any best-of-three on a radio show and no one could argue about the choice.

Growing up and embracing music in 1966 must have been a memorable experience. The choice was incredible and the possibilities endless.

One such young music fan was Mike Donovan. In 1966 he was a teenager in the St John's Wood area of London, a stone's throw from the Abbey Road recording studios made famous by The Beatles. Donovan, like so many of the generation who grew up with the music of the mid-Sixties, embraces it with just as much enthusiasm and interest four decades years later. He said:

It sounds a bit trite, I know, but I'm glad I grew up at that time mainly because of the pop culture. In the space of a few years we seemed to go from austere, stern-faced, post-war, black and white Britain to a time when anything was possible. It was like all the colours of the rainbow were being splashed across fashion, art, cinema, theatre and, for me and so many teenagers like me, music.

The stars shining brightest in the musical firmament, as they had throughout the first half of the Sixties, were, of course, The Beatles. However, The Beatles in 1966 were a very different band to the one which had emerged from Liverpool five years before and embarked on a seemingly unstoppable march towards world domination.

Nearly forty years on, *Sgt Pepper's Lonely Hearts Club Band*, which The Beatles began working on in November 1966 for release the following year, is still widely regarded as their *tour de force*. But *Revolver*, which came out at the beginning of August, a week after England's World Cup football triumph, was the album on which The Beatles finally cast aside the lovable mop-top image once and for all and seriously embraced musical experimentation like no band before. Four decades later, most discerning critics will tell you that *Revolver*, not *Sgt Pepper*, is the Beatles' recording which essentially defined what Lennon, McCartney, Harrison and Starr were all about.

Yet as a contradiction, perhaps no record of that time captured the mood of 'Swinging London' as well as *Revolver*, although The Rolling Stones had made a pretty decent stab at it earlier in the year with *Aftermath*. Meanwhile, Ray Davies was cementing his reputation as one of the decade's top songwriters with his continued excellence as leading light in The Kinks.

It had been a tumultuous eight months for The Beatles even before the release of *Revolver*. Their profile was probably at its peak, but by the end of the year, as the four members increasingly began to contemplate life beyond the constraints of the band, perhaps 1966 also marked the beginning of the end for them as the musical phenomenon of the decade.

In the year that Liverpool's Cavern Club, the venue forever synonymous with the group's formative years, closed down, they took the decision not to give any more live performances. Years of travel all around the world had taken their toll long before an increasingly frazzled foursome gave their final concert in San Francisco on 29 August at the end of the American leg of a worldwide tour which, with hindsight, was probably one trip too far.

The Beatles may have lost some of their popularity but they were still the biggest band in the world in 1966, with a huge fan base.
(*Redferns Music Picture Library*)

It had started to unravel in Manila a few weeks earlier after the dictatorial president's wife, Imelda Marcos, had laid on a lavish reception for 300 local worthies at the presidential palace. The invitation handed to Brian Epstein, the Beatles' manager, gave no hint of the preparations involved and the band, not surprisingly, stayed away. The next day Epstein pleaded to appear on the Philippines' state-run television to apologise for their no-show. Only then did the death threats stop.

The band's entourage were punched and kicked as they ran through the terminal at Manila airport towards the sanctuary of their aircraft, but the plane took off only after Epstein had paid a £7,000 sweetener to a government official. As they flew from New Delhi to London on the second leg of the journey home, the exhausted Beatles told Epstein that when the tour ended in America at the end of August there would be no more. Epstein was devastated at the time, although a fraught few weeks on the other side of the Atlantic probably convinced him that they had made the right decision after some careless comments to a newspaper reporter earlier in the year by John Lennon came back to haunt the band when they headed to the States in early August.

In March, Lennon had given one of his fairly regular interviews to the London *Evening Standard*. When asked for his views on organised religion, he responded: 'Christianity will go, it will vanish and shrink . . . we're more popular than Jesus now.' He had nothing against Jesus, he insisted, but the disciples were 'thick'. 'They're the ones that ruin it for me,' he added.

Tara Browne, heir to the Guinness fortune and a close friend of John Lennon, died in December when he drove his Lotus sports car into a lamp-post in London. Lennon remembered Browne in 'A Day in the Life' on The Beatles' 1967 album *Sgt Pepper's Lonely Hearts Club Band*.

Lennon's flippancy barely caused a stir in Britain, but when the interview was reproduced in a magazine aimed at impressionable American teenagers on the eve of the tour, Lennon's throwaway remarks had become: 'The Beatles were bigger than Jesus Christ.' From the moral majority in America, particularly the fundamentalist elements in the southern states, the outcry, inevitably, was long and loud.

Radio stations invited disillusioned youngsters to burn their Beatles albums, one community in Tennessee even placed rubbish bins labelled 'Beatles Trash Here' in the streets while a pastor in Ohio threatened to excommunicate anyone in his congregation who attended one of their concerts. More than thirty radio stations – most of them, it has to be said, south of the Mason-Dixon line – stopped playing their records. Even in Europe, Lennon's comments were denounced by everyone from the Pope to the Spanish government.

Another American controversy was only just averted. The sleeve of a compilation album, released by their stateside label Capitol and inspired by Lennon, showed the band in butcher's overalls, brandishing hunks of meat while they dismembered toy dolls. The outrage felt on both sides of the pond meant 750,000 copies of the offending album sleeve had to be recalled. Record label lackies spent an entire weekend putting the disc into a new sleeve which showed the band leaning against a trunk. In some cases, the new cover was simply pasted over the offending one.

At the beginning of August, Epstein arrived in America ahead of the band fearing the worst. He even offered to pay $1 million out of his own pocket to cancel the tour, but he was persuaded that it should go ahead. Lennon, who had

The Beatles leave for America for what would be their final tour in August 1966. *(Central Press/Getty Images)*

been receiving hate mail, looked more ashen-faced than usual as he apologised in Chicago when The Beatles arrived on 12 August, a week after the UK release of *Revolver*.

Not only was it their last, the American tour would also go down as the most turbulent in The Beatles' history. It was to be no triumphal march around a country which had embraced them almost as one of their own since their breakthrough there two years earlier. There was a terror threat from the Ku Klux Klan in Memphis when a firecracker was thrown on to the stage, fans were attacked by police in Los Angeles, while the band played on in Washington seemingly oblivious to the fact that serious race riots were taking place a few blocks away. In Cincinnati, they had to return the following day to appease 35,000 fans who had been sent home after a downpour flooded the open-air stage and the gig was postponed because of the risk of electrocution.

To his lasting regret, Epstein – who died the following year – missed their final concert at Candlestick Park, San Francisco. A briefcase of his containing, among other things, drugs, pornographic photographs and letters of a homosexual nature, had been stolen from his rented house in Beverly Hills and he was too scared to leave for fear that he and the Beatles would be blackmailed.

The band returned to the relative sanctuary of the UK to find *Revolver*, bolstered by advanced sales of one million, top of the charts and receiving critical acclaim. *Sgt Pepper* may have achieved more in homogeneity of sound, but *Revolver* was fresher and offered more variety than the Beatles' next release. It is still regarded as a classic.

Playing to the crowd. The Beatles in America, August 1966. *(Redferns Music Picture Library)*

Beatles' manager Brian Epstein missed the band's final concert in San Francisco, something he regretted for the rest of his life. *(Copyright © popperfoto.com)*

On the opening track, 'Taxman', George Harrison – who had married the actress Patti Boyd in January – took a satirical look at the increasing amount of the band's wealth which went to the Treasury. Paul McCartney was at his melancholy best on 'Eleanor Rigby' – the band's eleventh successive number one single – and there was a hint of The Beach Boys about 'Here, There and Everywhere' and 'Good Day Sunshine', both paeans to his girlfriend at the time, the English actress Jane Asher.

Then there was the unforgettable 'Yellow Submarine' – ostensibly a children's song which featured Ringo Starr on vocals as well as a brass band – while Lennon's vocal contributions included 'Your Bird Can Sing' and 'Dr Robert' – a tribute to the man who tended to the band's 'medicinal' needs. Lennon would later claim he couldn't remember whether *Revolver* came before *Sgt Pepper*, a statement not unconnected to the amount of LSD he was taking at the time. Nevertheless, his acid-fused imagination merged perfectly with McCartney's songwriting on the record.

The Beatles at the Beeb, June 1966. *(Redferns Music Picture Library)*

Mike Donovan remembers:

> It was hardly surprising, I suppose, that I was so keen on The Beatles, living so close to Abbey Road. One of my pals was Stuart Goddard (who earned fame and fortune fifteen years later as Adam Ant) and we would sit around miming to Beatles' records and copying their moves from the ITV show *Ready Steady Go!*
>
> Paul McCartney lived a few hundred yards away in Cavendish Place and there were always autograph hunters outside his gates, pretty much 24/7. McCartney-spotting was a local sport. I remember seeing him in a chocolate shop just down the road from National Radio which was where we bought our records.

As they basked in the success of *Revolver*, it was hard to believe that being in the most successful band of all time might not offer enough personal and professional satisfaction, but The Beatles were starting to stretch their wings even though, from the outside, the bond between the four of them seemed as strong as ever.

By the end of the year Lennon had appeared as Private Gripweed in his third film, the Richard Lester-directed (and financed) *How I Won the War*, which was partly filmed in Spain. His interest in the art world took him increasingly to fashionable London galleries. In November, at the Indica, he became fascinated by an exhibition called 'Unfinished Paintings and Objects' by a Japanese-born

By the end of 1966 John Lennon was exploring other artistic avenues and had made his third film.
(Express/Getty Images)

American already enjoying a little notoriety in London for a photo-
graphic exhibition of nude bottoms. He had to meet her and he did. The artist
was Yoko Ono.

It was a great time to embrace musical experimentation and The Beatles were
by no means the only band who wanted to try something different.

Surprisingly perhaps, given that they had established their reputation as out
and out rockers, plenty of it could be found on 'Paint It Black', a number one
single in May and a standout track on *Aftermath*, the fourth studio album by
The Rolling Stones. For the first time, the Stones revealed themselves as much
more than a group able to successfully fuse R&B with conventional pop music.
It was also their first album made up entirely of Keith Richards and Mick
Jagger compositions.

Lyrically they were as sharp as ever. The opening number, 'Mother's Little
Helper', was a sarcastic put-down on the valium abuse of suburban housewives
and contrasted sharply with the Elizabethan-style love song 'Lady Jane',
complete with Brian Jones on atmospheric dulcimer.

There was evidence of the band's deep-rooted misogyny, particularly on the
confident 'Under My Thumb', while the Stones maintained their run of singles
successes with the marvellously chaotic '19th Nervous Breakdown' and its
scale-sliding guitar.

Nasty to The Beatles' nice. In 1966 you either loved the Rolling Stones or hated them.
(Redferns Music Picture Library)

Mike Donovan remembers:

> The Stones were projected as nasty to The Beatles' nice at the time. You either liked one or the other.
>
> The Stones interpreted American rhythm and blues superbly but they also developed their own song-writing talents at the time. I think The Stones lost something when they were suddenly regarded as the best rock 'n' roll band in the world rather than interpreters of R&B artists like Jimmy Reed and original rock 'n' roll like Chuck Berry.

The Stones' writing potential was underlined still further when Chris Farlowe topped the charts with one of their compositions, 'Out Of Time', which was produced by Jagger.

By 1966 newspapers may have stopped asking 'Would You Let Your Daughter Marry a Rolling Stone?', but controversy was never far away, particularly when the Stones embarked on lengthy tours. Not that they seemed to be too bothered by any fuss.

In January a local promoter was fined £1,200 when the authorities in Munich decreed that the Stones had simply made 'noise' rather than 'music' at a concert in the West German city. Two months later eighty-five fans were arrested and ten gendarmes injured in Paris when a 2,500-strong crowd rioted. Back in Germany in September the *Daily Mirror* claimed the band had unleashed a 'typhoon of destruction' after fans rioted at the start of another European tour. The Stones lapped it up. A fortnight later they began the British leg of the tour at the Albert Hall supported by The Yardbirds and Ike and Tina Turner.

American audiences loved them, too, although the authorities over there were a bit more po-faced. In Syracuse they were accused of dragging the Stars and Stripes across a concert hall, while their reputation was such that fourteen hotels in New York turned down their patronage. The band filed a £1.7 million lawsuit, claiming that the hotels had damaged their reputation.

It may have appeared that other bands were living in the perpetual shadow of both the Beatles and the Stones, but the UK charts were full of home-grown groups and solo artists establishing strong reputations of their own.

Beat-boom contemporaries were still popular and arguably the most successful in 1966 were Manfred Mann. Paul Jones's harmonica-playing helped to give their sound a distinctive edge and they scored a number one in May with 'Pretty Flamingo', although this was the last hit on which Jones appeared before embarking on a solo career – a move which wasn't received well at a time when fans loathed personnel changes in their favourite groups. Incidentally, Rod Stewart failed the audition when the band came to recruit Jones's replacement.

'Keep On Running' had given The Spencer Davis Group a breakthrough hit in 1965 and the following year, propelled in no small part by Steve Winwood's mercurial talent, they maintained their success with another chart-topper, 'Somebody Help Me' (number one for two weeks in April), and two albums, *The Second Album* and *Autumn '66*.

Meanwhile, Ray Davies was beginning to forge a song-writing reputation as strong as that of Lennon and McCartney. Disputes among band members meant The Kinks may have appeared ready to implode at any time, but Davies seemed to be able to rise above all the internal strife as a thought-provoking lyricist of originality, humour and pathos who penned a string of successful singles in the mid-Sixties.

Revolver could lay strong claim to have been the album which epitomised 'Swinging London' in 1966, but surely the singles which captured the prevailing mood at the time were Davies compositions. 'Sunny Afternoon', which dealt with capitalism and the class system, reached number one the week after England's Wembley triumph, and, at the end of the year, 'Dead End Street' highlighted the problems still facing the working classes: 'Out of work and got no money, a Sunday joint of bread and honey.' It was delivered in a melancholy style which remains instantly recognisable four decades later. Both were included on *Face to Face*, the album which, above all others, showcased his unique songwriting talents and was released in 1966.

Davies is regarded as one of the four best English songwriters of that period. Completing that impressive quartet, alongside Lennon and McCartney, was Pete Townshend, who was establishing his reputation in The Who. Townshend's anthem for disaffected youth, 'My Generation', had provided The Who with their breakthrough in 1965 and the following year they released 'A Quick One'. By now the band were establishing themselves as one of the best live acts around as well.

It was the halcyon period for British Mods. Yet only The Who and The Small Faces could claim commercial success during 1965 and 1966. But Mod music provided the link between the beat boom bands and British psychedelia which was to emerge the following year. The sound typified British pop at its most ebullient and effervescent.

The outcry over Lennon's anti-Christ remarks added to an increasing disenchantment among American audiences over the music which was coming from the other side of the Atlantic. The enthusiasm for early-year Beatles and the bands who beat a triumphal path in their wake was starting to wane. In their place, The Rolling Stones and The Who seemed to stand for a generation of

Pete Townshend had established himself as one of the best songwriters of his generation. *(Redferns Music Picture Library)*

The Who on the road again. The mid-Sixties were halcyon days for British Mods. *(Redferns Music Picture Library)*

British bands whose music lacked appeal to less liberal-thinking Stateside audiences.

American artists, seemingly galvanised into action by the Beatles-led invasion of a few years earlier, started to hit back. Their music wasn't about high school sweethearts, five and dimes and drive-in movies any more. Forget Bobby Vee and Pat Boone. Instead, Bob Dylan, Joan Baez and bands like The Byrds held up their own country to ridicule with songs about the Vietnam War, racism and even the prospect of impending nuclear doom. They sold by the millions and in 1966 British audiences began to embrace their message and, in Dylan's case, a love of the mouth-organ solo.

The musicians on *Blonde on Blonde*, who included Robbie Robertson and Al Kooper, responded to Dylan's demand for improvisation while he produced some of his finest vocal performances. *Blonde on Blonde* was also one of his most ambitious projects to date. 'Sad-Eyed Lady of the Lowlands' was eleven minutes and nineteen seconds long. You could have squeezed four tracks from *Revolver* into the same time.

Dylan embarked on a UK tour in late spring which his fans lapped up. Until he got to the Manchester Free Trade Hall on 17 May, that is. The first part of his show, performed acoustic and solo, had gone down well even though the messages contained in his lyrics were not as socially conscious or politically motivated as those which had gained Dylan so much popularity earlier in the decade.

Now he stood in a hound's-tooth suit with pointed boots in front of a five-piece band with an electric guitar in his hand and proceeded to play good old-fashioned rock 'n' roll.

His fans couldn't believe what they were seeing – or hearing. Their hero had 'sold out'. Just before the last number someone shouted, 'Judas', to which Dylan replied, 'I don't believe you.' He turned his back on the audience, turned to his band and shouted, 'Play fuckin' loud!'

They did, launching into a rousing version of 'Like a Rolling Stone', Dylan's voice sneering 'How does it feeeel' to an increasingly bemused audience.

For years the identity of the Judas 'shouter' remained a mystery. Several people claimed to have harangued Dylan at the Free Trade Hall that night but the most credible was Keith Butler, who was studying at Keele University at the time.

C.P. Lee's book about the concert, published in 1998, and the publicity it attracted caused several potential 'shouters' to come forward and Butler, who was living in Canada at the time, did so after hearing about the book on a radio programme. He can clearly be seen criticising Dylan in the film of the concert, *Eat The Document*, which included footage of the audience leaving the concert after the show.

Electric Blues. Bob Dylan stunned his Manchester audience when he turned to his band and shouted: 'Play fuckin' loud.' *(Redferns Music Picture Library)*

There was even a reunion in 1999 of people who were there that night at the Free Trade Hall and several, including Butler and C.P. Lee, were interviewed by Andy Kershaw for a documentary, *Ghosts of Electricity*, which was broadcast the same year. Butler died of cancer three years later.

Entertainment Weekly summed up Dylan's performance and that of his band thus: 'From the snarl of Robbie Robertson's guitar to the carnival-carousel tone of Garth Hudson's organ to the prodding sneer of Dylan's voice, it's a joyful mess, reflecting Dylan's own precarious mental health and his need to leave the folk ghetto.'

Bootleg copies of that concert remain one of the most sought-after recordings for collectors four decades later.

In July Dylan's seemingly non-stop round of touring and recording was brought to an abrupt end by a near-fatal motorcycle accident in California. He remained out of the public limelight for the next two years.

While *Sgt Pepper* was hailed as a technological breakthrough when it was released the following year, as much musical innovation could be found in 1966 on *Pet Sounds*, ostensibly a Beach Boys' record but every much the immaculate conception of troubled band founder Brian Wilson. Here was a record of intensely personal recordings brimming with inventive arrangements. Taking their inspiration not from *Revolver*, but The Beatles' 1965 release *Rubber Soul*, it was so unlike anything the band had released before and was received with far greater enthusiasm in Britain than America where the reaction was, at best, lukewarm. It only just scraped into the *Billboard* top ten.

'I was obsessed with explaining, musically, how I felt inside,' Wilson remarked some years later. 'I thought this could be the beginning of a new type of sophisticated-feeling music.

'During the production of *Pet Sounds*, I dreamt I had a halo over my head. This might have meant the angels were watching over *Pet Sounds*.'

All very deep and meaningful, of course, but Wilson could doubtless never have imagined that one of the tracks, 'Sloop John B', would be adopted by British rugby players everywhere many years later . . . as their favourite drinking song. By the end of the year, however, The Beach Boys had returned to form in their home market with the release of another smash-hit single, 'Good Vibrations'.

To be growing up and embracing music at this time, as teenagers like Mike Donovan were, was an experience which makes him go dewy-eyed even today, four decades later:

> Money was tight so myself and my mates would form a three-way syndicate to buy an album a week. Singles were more affordable. The 'big' single of the week would always be in the window of National Radio, proudly displayed and especially if it was a Beatles' single in its green Parlophone jacket.

Good Vibrations. The Beach Boys'
Pet Sounds was a huge hit with
British fans although it was less
popular back home in America.
(Redferns Music Picture Library)

We knew *Revolver* was something different from the sleeve artwork and the fact that John (Lennon) was photographed in a flowery shirt with long hair. We thought it was Britain's first psychedelic album. As always, they led the way.

We loved The Beatles, but I have to say that just below them stood Jimi Hendrix and, later in the year, Cream. Eric Clapton was 'God', we were in awe of him. I can still remember seeing him on *Ready Steady Go!* performing Hey Joe. Eventually, at school or when you were on the street with your mates, you were either Hendrix or Cream. Once it had been the Beatles or the Stones.

Cream lasted barely two years and released just four albums, but for a generation they are still regarded as the world's first supergroup.

Eric Clapton had been expelled from art college for playing his guitar in class. Eventually he drifted into manual labouring work but eventually found himself in two bands which would become renowned as nurseries for a generation of British guitar greats: John Mayall's Bluesbreakers and The Yardbirds.

He first ran into Ginger Baker at a Bluesbreakers' gig in Oxfordshire in 1966 when Baker was drumming for a jazz-blues band called The Graham Bond Organisation. Baker was enthralled by Clapton's guitar playing and suggested they form a band after seducing Clapton with the offer of a lift in his Rover, in those days one of the most desirable cars on the road.

The band was nearly scuppered there and then when Clapton suggested they recruit Jack Bruce, a one-time boy soprano and now bass player in The Graham Bond Organisation. There was no doubting Bruce's talent, but he and Baker disliked each other intensely.

Baker thought Bruce's playing too ostentatious and he would often throw drumsticks at the back of his head during rehearsals and concerts. Bruce once hurled a guitar at his fellow band member and the pair often had fist fights. Once, a knife was pulled.

But from this obvious creative tension, and with Clapton in the mix, there came some improbable magic. After making their debut at the Windsor Jazz and Blues Festival in late summer, Cream took off. The name was Clapton's idea and suggested their rich fusion of sounds. In reality, it was his subtle way of saying that each member of the trio was to be regarded as the best in their field. Their first album, *Fresh Cream*, made an instant impression. Mike Donovan recalls:

I remember trying to belt out the words to 'Sweet Wine' (from *Fresh Cream*) wearing a jumper my mother had knitted for me in a church hall in Belsize Park. Gary Grainger, who went on to play lead guitar in Rod Stewart's band, was watching. He didn't look impressed!

The world's first supergoup? Cream were establishing a considerable reputation by the end of 1966. (Copyright © popperfcto.com)

MUSICAL MILESTONES IN 1966

January

- The BBC premiered its new music show, *A Whole Scene Going*. Guests on the first programme included The Who, Lulu and Spike Milligan.
- The Overlanders topped the singles chart for three weeks with their version of The Beatles' hit, 'Michelle'. Among those denied the number one spot by its success were Crispian St Peters with 'You Were on my Mind' and 'A Groovy Kind of Love' by The Mindbenders, both of which were stuck at number two.
- The Swinging Blue Jeans made the chart for the last time with 'Don't Make Me Over', while 'Keep on Running' gave The Spencer Davis Group the first of two top-selling singles in 1966.
- Close harmony trio The Ivy League, who had had three top-thirty hits in 1965, announced that Tony Burroughs was replacing founder member John Carter while The Merseybeats split after 'I Stand Accused' only reached no. 38 in the singles chart.
- Pye record label cancelled the release of Donovan's *Sunshine Superman* in a row over distribution with its producer, Micky Most. It eventually came out in December.

The prolific Spencer Davis group released two big-selling albums in 1966. *(Redferns Music Picture Library)*

February

- The Rolling Stones released their new single, '19th Nervous Breakdown', but it was kept off the top of the singles chart by Nancy Sinatra's 'These Boots Are Made For Walking'. Also in the top five were The Small Faces' 'Sha La La La Lee' and Petula Clark's double A-side 'My Love'/'Where Am I Going', which did top the American singles chart for two weeks.
- Sinatra also kept The Hollies' 'I Can't Let Go' off top spot while producer/manager Larry Page agreed a five-year recording contract with The Troggs.
- The price of a 45rpm single rose by 7*d* to 7*s* 3*d* (36 pence) while American soul singer James Brown made his first appearance on ITV's *Ready Steady Go!*. The Four Pennies' 'Trouble is my Middle Name' reached no. 32 and was their last chart success.
- Peter and Gordon's career was undoubtedly enhanced by the patronage of Paul McCartney, who was going out with Peter Asher's sister. They reached no. 28 with 'Woman'.
- The Musicians Union proposed that miming be banned from television shows while Pink Floyd heralded the arrival the British underground scene by beginning their bi-weekly residency, complete with psychedelic light show, at London's Marquee Club.

March

- The BBC showed a recording of the Beatles' concert at Shea Stadium on the 1st, and the month began with The Walker Brothers' 'The Sun Ain't Gonna Shine Anymore' at the top of the singles chart.
- Also in the top five were The Yardbirds' 'Shape of Things to Come', 'Hold Tight' by Dave, Dee, Dozy, Beaky, Mick and Tich and 'Dedicated Follower of Fashion', the Kinks' paean to Carnaby Street.
- The Kinks were on tour without lead singer Ray Davies, who was ill at home in London suffering from flu. But on 17 March he still managed to find the energy to run from his home in Fortis Green to central London to physically attack manager Brian Somerville who, not surprisingly, resigned from the band's organisation the following day.
- The Spencer Davis Group topped the charts for the second time in the year with 'Somebody Help Me', while The Who were forced to release their single 'Substitute', which reached no. 5, through their own label after a judge served an injunction on Polydor following a law suit brought by producer Shel Talmy. The case was settled out of court, but Talmy retained royalty rights on all the band's recordings for the remainder of the Sixties.

- Cliff Richard was back in the singles charts with 'Blue Turns to Grey', while among the month's album releases were *The Best of the Animals*, Herman's Hermits' *Listen People* and *Try Too Hard* by The Dave Clark Five, a beat band enjoying considerably more success in America where they had seventeen successive *Billboard* chart hits.

April
- Manfred Mann replaced The Spencer Davis Group, who had embarked on a joint tour with The Who, at the top of the singles' chart with 'Pretty Flamingo'.
- The Rolling Stones' new album *Aftermath* went straight to number one and they had an American top-selling single later in the month with 'Paint It Black'. Meanwhile, back in London, The Lovin' Spoonful made their UK live debut at the Marquee Club.
- Johnny Kidd disbanded The Pirates after the release of 'It's Gotta Be You', while Pinkerton's Assorted Colours charted for the last time with 'Don't Stop Lovin' Me Baby'.
- Dusty Springfield replaced Manfred Mann at the top of the charts for a week with 'You Don't Have to Say You Love Me'.
- Cilla Black reached no. 9 with the title track to the new Michael Caine movie, *Alfie*, and in London Eric Clapton began recording with John Mayall and the Bluesbreakers at Decca Records' studio in West Hampstead.

May
- The line-up of the year assembled at the Empire Pool, Wembley, for the NME Poll Winners' party. Among the artists who performed were The Beatles, The Rolling Stones, The Walker Brothers, The Who, Spencer Davis Group, The Yardbirds and Herman's Hermits.
- In Bristol, on 10 May, Bob Dylan opened his second UK tour, introducing a rock backing band, the Hawks, for the second part of his show. The tour culminated at the Royal Albert Hall on the 26th.
- In the charts, The Stones' 'Paint it Black' replaced 'Pretty Flamingo' as number one single, Keith Richards purchased the Redlands estate in West Sussex and *Aftermath* was released in the States. The Beatles' 'Paperback Writer' went straight to the top of the American chart. The Troggs were stuck at no. 2 with 'Wild Thing' while other top twenty artists during the month included Ken Dodd, who reached no. 6 with 'Promises'.

June

- The Kinks were never far from the headlines during the month. When bassist Peter Quaife was injured in a car accident on the 5th, he was replaced six days later by John Dalton. Dalton was then jailed by Madrid police after local promoters complained that not all of the contracted band members were appearing in a show. They refused to pay and also confiscated the group's equipment. And at the same time 'Sunny Afternoon' was released, and would eventually reach no. 1. Frank Sinatra had been there for three weeks in June with a re-issue of 'Strangers In The Night' before he was replaced by The Beatles' 'Paperback Writer'.
- Twice As Much had their only UK chart entry when 'Sittin' on a Fence' reached no. 25. Among the more established chart acts in June were The Hollies with 'Bus Stop' and 'Over Under Sideways Down' by The Yardbirds.
- Eric Clapton, Ginger Baker and Jack Bruce announced plans to form Cream, singer Paul Jones confirmed he was leaving Manfred Mann while the Musicians Union successfully closed down shows where the artists mimed to their hits.
- Cliff Richard made an appearance at Billy Graham's crusade in London and the pirate station Radio City, which broadcast from the Thames Estuary, closed down after its owner Reg Calvert, who also managed several Sixties bands, got involved in a dispute over the ownership of its transmitter with rival promoter Sir Oliver Smedley. When Calvert went to confront Smedley at his Essex home the following day, he was shot dead.

July

- On the day of England's greatest footballing triumph, Chris Farlowe was top of the charts with 'Out Of Time', one of three number ones in the month. 'Sunny Afternoon' became The Kinks' third chart-topper before they were replaced by Georgie Fame and the Blue Flames with 'Get Away'. Within a few days Fame and his backing band split.
- On the day of the World Cup final, The Who topped the bill on the second day of the sixth Windsor Jazz and Blues Festival. Headliners on the first day were the Spencer Davis Group and The Small Faces. Cream played on the final day when the bill was topped by Georgie Fame and The Blue Flames.
- John Mayall and Eric Clapton's *Bluesbreakers* had its UK release. Other notable album releases in the month included *From Nowhere*, by The Troggs. Meanwhile, the *Sound of Music* soundtrack was in the middle of another seven-week residency at the top of the UK album chart.

August

- The Beatles' double A side, 'Yellow Submarine'/'Eleanor Rigby', followed *Revolver* straight to the top of the singles and album chart, a week before the band embarked on their final tour of the US. The single had replaced The Troggs' 'A Girl Like You' at number one. The Beatles performed to 44,000 in New York's Shea Stadium – 11,000 fewer fans than in 1965.
- The Tremeloes went in search of commercial success with their version of 'Good Day Sunshine', from *Revolver*, while Napoleon XIV – the pseudonym of songwriter and recording engineer Jerry Samuels – had the novelty top ten hit of 1966 with 'They're Coming to Take Me Away, Ha Ha'.

September

- On the 24th Jimi Hendrix arrived in London, went straight to a jam session and five days later auditioned Noel Redding for his new band. Meanwhile, Eric Burdon left The Animals at the end of their American tour and John Dalton was confirmed as permanent replacement for Peter Quaife in The Kinks.
- In the singles chart, The Small Faces took over from The Beatles for a week with 'All or Nothing'. They were replaced by Jim Reeves, who topped the chart for five weeks with 'Distant Drums'. Among other top ten artists in the month were The New Vaudeville Band with 'Winchester Cathedral', while Peter and Gordon, David Garrick and Crispian St Peters all entered the UK charts for the last time.
- Donovan had a US no. 1 album with *Sunshine Superman* and Pink Floyd played All Saints Church Hall in Notting Hill, London. Album releases in the month included *Animalization* by The Animals and The Yardbirds.

October

- A big month for Jimi Hendrix. Chas Chandler and Mike Jeffries were confirmed as his new co-managers and he eventually signed to new label Track Records after Kit Lambert and Chris Stamp heard him play at the Scotch of St James club in London. Mitch Mitchell quit Georgie Fame to team up with Hendrix's new band.
- Jeff Beck quit The Yardbirds during their tour because of persistent ill-health, according to his management, and was replaced by Jimmy Page. Johnny Kidd was killed in a car accident and Alma Cogan died of cancer at the age of 34.

- In the charts, *Revolver* was replaced at no. 1 album by the *Sound of Music* soundtrack while The Four Tops took over at the top of the singles chart on the 25th with 'Reach Out I'll Be There', keeping Manfred Mann's 'Semi-detached Suburban Mr James' off the no. 1 spot.
- Cream's first single, 'Wrapping Paper'/'Cats Squirrel' charted at no. 34 while The Moody Blues released their last album before the arrival of Justin Hayward with *Boulevard de la Madeleine*. Pink Floyd and The Soft Machine performed at a party in London to launch the *International Times* newspaper.

November

- The Beach Boys opened their UK tour on the 6th in London with Lulu among the support and a number one single with 'Good Vibrations'. Four days later Tom Jones released 'The Green, Green Grass of Home', which replaced 'Good Vibrations' on the 29th and remained at the top of the chart for the rest of the year.
- The latest instalment in the soap opera otherwise known as The Kinks saw the return of Peter Quaife on bass. John Dalton returned to his day job. The BBC banned the film accompanying their new single, 'Dead End Street', claiming it is in bad taste. It still reached no. 5.
- The Jimi Hendrix Experience played their first official UK gig at The Bag O'Nails in London. *New Musical Express* reported that Steve Winwood and Spencer Davis were no longer on speaking terms. Winwood left early in 1967 to form Traffic.

December

- *Ready Steady Go!* was broadcast by ITV for the last time on the 23rd. Eight days later BBC1 premiered The Monkees.
- The New Vaudeville Band had a surprise US number one for three weeks with 'Winchester Cathedral', while Tom Jones's month-long residency at the top of the UK chart kept Donovan's 'Sunshine Superman', taken from his new album *Mellow Yellow*, and 'Happy Jack', by The Who, off the coveted Christmas number one spot.
- Other album releases included Cream's *Fresh Cream* and *Night of Fear* by The Move.
- The Who and Pink Floyd headlined an all-night New Year's Eve rave at London's Roundhouse. At the same venue the previous night Geno Washington and the Ramjam Band topped the bill at the Giant Freakout Ball.

Tom Jones had the Christmas number one with 'The Green, Green Grass of Home'.
(McKeown/Getty Images)

Number One Albums

1 Jan–19 Feb: *Rubber Soul* – The Beatles (Parlophone)
19 Feb–30 Apr: *Sound of Music* soundtrack (RCA)
30 Apr–25 Jun: *Aftermath* – The Rolling Stones (Decca)
25 Jun–13 Aug: *Sound of Music* soundtrack
13 Aug–1 Oct: *Revolver* – The Beatles (Parlophone)
1 Oct–4 Feb 1967:   *Sound of Music* soundtrack

The *Sound of Music* soundtrack spent thirty-one weeks at the top of the British album charts in 1966. It had been top for twenty weeks in 1965 and its popularity didn't waver as the decade wore on. It was number one again for a further seven weeks in 1967 and even had another week at the top in 1968. The film also won Best Picture at the 1966 Oscars.

Number One Singles

4 Jan   (5 weeks): 'Day Tripper'/'We Can Work it Out' – The Beatles
18 Jan   (1 week):   'Keep on Running' – The Spencer Davis Group
25 Jan   (1 week):   'Michelle' – Overlanders
15 Feb   (4 weeks): 'These Boots Are Made For Walking' – Nancy Sinatra
15 Mar   (4 weeks): 'The Sun Ain't Gonna Shine Anymore' – Walker Brothers
12 Apr   (2 weeks): 'Somebody Help Me' – The Spencer Davis Group
26 Apr   (1 week):   'You Don't Have to Say You Love Me' – Dusty Springfield
3 May   (3 weeks): 'Pretty Flamingo' – Manfred Mann
24 May   (1 week):   'Paint it Black' – The Rolling Stones
31 May   (3 weeks): 'Stranger In The Night' – Frank Sinatra
21 June   (2 weeks): 'Paperback Writer' – The Beatles
5 July   (2 weeks): 'Sunny Afternoon' – The Kinks
19 July   (1 week):   'Get Away' – Georgie Fame and The Blue Flames
26 July   (1 week):   'Out of Time' – Chris Farlowe
2 Aug   (2 weeks): 'With a Girl Like You' – The Troggs
16 Aug   (4 weeks): 'Yellow Submarine'/'Eleanor Rigby' – The Beatles
13 Sep   (1 week):   'All or Nothing' – The Small Faces
20 Sep   (5 weeks): 'Distant Drums' – Jim Reeves
25 Oct   (3 weeks): 'Reach Out, I'll Be There' – The Four Tops
15 Nov   (2 weeks): 'Good Vibrations' – The Beach Boys
29 Nov   (7 weeks): 'The Green, Green Grass of Home' – Tom Jones

3

MARY, MODELS AND
THE MINI

In 1966 *Time* magazine described London as a city 'pulsating with half a dozen separate veins of excitement. . . . In this century every decade has its city . . . and for the Sixties that city is London.'

The capital was doing its best to live up to its star billing and London had taken over from Paris as the fashion centre of the world. At the heart of its thriving scene were three streets right in the middle of the metropolis. The King's Road had its own queen in Mary Quant; Church Street in Kensington had been put on the map by Barbara Hulanicki's 'total look' boutique Biba; and Carnaby Street had been transformed from a run-down alley behind Regent Street into the place where the young and cool congregated. They went merely to be seen as well as be clothed by designers such as John Stephen, a Scot who opened his first boutique selling pink hipsters and who decided that men's fashions should be as funky as women's.

London's Carnaby Street. The place to shop and be seen. (*John Waterman/Fox Photos/ Getty Images*)

Four decades ago fashion designers such as Mary Quant, the unofficial queen of 'Swinging London', were as instantly recognisable as the stars of pop music and films who were queuing up to wear her creations.

It was also the year that the supermodel phenomenon was born. Leslie Hornby burst into the British consciousness for the first time after she was declared 'The Face of 1966' by the *Daily Express* in February. You might know her better as Twiggy. Jean Shrimpton or 'The Shrimp' (a nickname she hated) was at the height of her fame in 1966, her distinctive features and classical beauty appealing in equal measure to both women and men.

Hemlines continued to rise, so much so that on 1 January the government brought in new rules to stop the increasing number of women who were avoiding paying taxes by buying their clothes in children's sizes. Remember, you could never be too thin (or too rich) in 1966. The 10 per cent levy which was imposed depended on the length of the clothes, although a re-think eventually resulted in women's clothes being measured by bust size instead.

Miniskirts eventually became microskirts. But nothing stayed the same for too long. By the end of the year, with the flower power era just around the corner, ruffles, bosoms, waists, lockets and ribbons were suddenly the look. For men, ties were out and open-necked shirts, swept-back hair, sideburns and velvet collars became *de rigueur*.

The novelist Julian Barnes recalled: 'I was at Oxford in 1966. I wore my hair long and had a pair of purple jeans which were excruciatingly uncomfortable at the crotch.' He wasn't alone. Fashion could sometimes be hard work.

As 1967 dawned fashion may have been yearning for a bygone era yet a French designer, Pierre Cardin, had already gone back to the future with mini dresses made out of metal plates accessorised with chain-link belts and heavy metal necklaces.

It was a time of paper dresses and even paper underwear. The American-based Scott Paper Company introduced a paper dress which retailed at just over a dollar in 1966. It was meant to be nothing more than a publicity stunt, but within six months they had sold more than half a million dresses. The company soon discovered, however, that conventional dress production cost little more and disposable clothes disappeared as quickly as they arrived. The paper underwear didn't catch on either. I wonder why.

Go-Go boots lasted a little longer, and at the same time one-piece tights were proving popular. Stockings and suspenders eventually made a comeback, but in 1966, as hemlines rose, they were virtually obsolete as women showed off their legs.

The most popular items of jewellery were gypsy-hoop earrings. 'Do you know any teenager who isn't wearing them?' asked the *Daily Telegraph* in March. 'The new enamel or plastic ones in brilliant sugar colours to match one's dress are pulling crowds into the stores. They give a necessary feminine touch to a girl whose hair is cropped shorter than her escort's.'

For a generation of Britons brought up on clothes rationing after the Second World War, not a lot appeared to have changed. They still wore sensible clothes and had sensible haircuts. But their children did have a choice. Forty years ago the majority of school-leavers went straight into employment rather than further education. They had plenty of disposable income and the commercial manufacturers soon realised that young people were happy to spend it following the latest trends.

Dedicated followers of fashion. London was the place to be and be seen in 1966. *(Ray Roberts/Getty Images)*

But while London may have been 'swinging' it wasn't necessarily the case in other areas of the country. Miniskirts? In a lot of provincial England and elsewhere in Britain most people hadn't even heard of them, let alone worn them. Although the influence of London fashion would eventually permeate the rest of the country it took some time, for instance, before you could stroll into a men's boutique outside of the capital and buy yourself a fur coat off the peg.

THE SUPERMODELS

Twiggy

Twiggy was born Lesley Hornby in north London in 1949. Having learned to sew at an early age, she was soon making her own clothes and taking an interest in fashion. Her life changed in 1965 when, at the age of 15 and still at school, she met hairdresser Nigel Davis, a man ten years her elder who worked in a hair salon with his brother Tony and had already established himself as one of the decade's leading crimpers.

It was Tony Davis who gave Lesley her nickname because of her toothpick-thin, six-and-a-half stone frame. First she was called 'Sticks', then 'Twigs' and finally 'Twiggy'. 'I was really skinny,' she said. 'But I was healthy – although if I'd had a fairy godmother I would have wanted to look like Brenda Lee, you know, very shapely.'

Tony's brother decided on a name change as well. Fed up with plain old Nigel Davis, he became the much more exotic Justin de Villeneuve, and by 1966 he had become Twiggy's manager as well as her boyfriend. Justin had initially considered going into the garment business but Twiggy remembers how her own life changed in January 1966 when she was transformed from schoolgirl to supermodel.

'Justin took me to Leonard's salon in Mayfair for about seven hours and they were cutting and colouring my hair. It was all extremely exciting for me. Leonard (or Len Lewis, to give him his proper name) was brilliant. I went from this mouse-like brown to the colour which I have kept now. After the haircut I got the bus to the studio of Barry Lategan, the photographer.'

Lategan has photographed Twiggy many times since, but still remembers that first session:

> She appeared with this short haircut which was an extraordinary transformation in her because her face came out more prominently and she had a beautifully modelled face.
>
> There was something new to me because she had painted her own eyelashes below her eye which was something no one had done before. She sat in front of the camera and it was dazzling.

Twiggy and her manager and boyfriend, Justin de Villeneuve. *(Ted West/Central Press/Getty Images)*

We photographed her side on. Leonard changed her hair into a curl, put a plait in it and smoothed her hair away. Just different ways to show this haircut. There are so many adjectives to describe what photogenic actually is, but my photos of Twiggy show the result of that. A few days later I made the prints and Leonard displayed them in his salon as usual.

The face of 1966: Twiggy. *(Stan Meagher/Getty Images)*

Twiggy remembers what happened next. 'Deidre McSharry, of the *Daily Express*, saw them and said: "Who is this girl?" Anyway, she phoned us and we went along to her office and she wrote this big article on me which appeared in the paper. It all happened from there really.'

On 23 February the paper introduced 'The Cockney kid with a face to launch a thousand shapes . . . and she's only 16!' A star was born.

With her 32-22-32 figure and boyish, waif-like looks accentuated by her new haircut, Twiggy became an overnight success. By the end of the year she had launched her own clothing range aimed at the teenage market, called Twiggy Dresses, and was about to make an even bigger impact in America where she soon established a huge fan base. On her debut appearance on *The Johnny Carson Show*, she had to escape from the mob of onlookers outside by leaving through the garbage chute.

She even had time to record her first single, 'Beautiful Dreams'. Within months of Lategan's photo shoot she had become one of the country's highest earners, commanding fees of ten guineas (£10.50 in modern currency) an hour. In addition to her modelling and clothing line she had a boutique in the King's Road, a film processing shop and even her own brand of knitting machines.

By 1970 her modelling days were over. She concentrated instead on an acting career during which she made fifteen films, the most famous of which was probably Ken Russell's *The Boyfriend*, a clever pastiche based on a Twenties musical. She also had a productive theatrical and television career, which is still flourishing, and although she was perhaps less successful as a recording artist she did produce a critically-acclaimed album of her favourite tunes from the previous two decades as recently as 2003.

But Twiggy the model is how most people will always remember her. Four decades after her breakthrough she is still adorning the pages of mail order clothing catalogues and modelling for Marks & Spencer. Yet she insists she is not a model and says she doesn't really follow current fashion trends. In 2004, she said: 'People always ask me about my time as a model, but I really don't think of myself like that. I think of myself as a dancer and actress.

'I did love fashion! At school I was terribly insecure. I was very thin and flat-chested. I wasn't good at anything but I did love fashion. I used to dream about being a designer, so when I was a model I really enjoyed the clothes.'

Jean Shrimpton

In contrast to the emerging superstar, Jean Shrimpton was something of an old hand but throughout the decade Shrimpton remained the world's most famous model. In 1966, she was at the peak of her career.

Born in High Wycombe in 1942, Shrimpton was the most famous name to emerge from the Lucie Clayton Model Agency. Throughout the Sixties Lucie Clayton models ruled the worlds of fashion and showbusiness. They may famously have turned down Twiggy because she wanted to bring de Villeneuve with her as manager, but Shrimpton, Jackie Collins, Shirley Ann Field, Joanna Lumley and Sandra Paul (these days the wife of former Conservative Party leader Michael Howard) all enjoyed successful modelling careers thanks to Lucie Clayton.

Leslie Kark, who took over the agency in 1950 with his wife Evelyn, recalled the impact of his organisation's biggest success story. 'Jean was a doctor's daughter, a very fine girl. We had to spend a lot of time guarding her from Terence Stamp (with whom Shrimpton had an intense affair throughout 1966) and David Bailey.'

Shrimpton's modelling career took off in 1962 with her first *Vogue* shoot. Four years later she reached her peak after signing a three-year contract to promote Yardley's Londonderry range of hair products. In contrast to Twiggy, she weighed 120 pounds and her 32-23-35 figure could best be described as robust. Her younger sister, Chrissie, was Mick Jagger's girlfriend in 1966 before the Rolling Stone was swept off his feet by Marianne Faithfull.

Jean herself thought she suffered from 'a fat face, a weak left profile, small eyes, big feet and bags under her eyes'. 'If you take off the make-up, I'm ugly,' she said. And she hated dressing up. The Shrimp claimed to own just one evening dress during her modelling career. Usually she wore skirts she had knitted herself and would turn up to shoots in an old sweater or in one of the five dresses she is reputed to have owned at the height of her fame in 1966. 'I can't bear being dressed up,' she said.

Jean Shrimpton. 'She had a kind of democratic beauty,' according to photographer David Bailey. *(Getty Images)*

Her disparaging view of the way she looked was not shared by many, least of all Bailey who was establishing himself, along with Terence Donovan and Brian Duffy, as one of the leading London fashion photographers forty years ago. They were nicknamed 'the terrible trio'.

It was Bailey, according to the legendary photographer Cecil Beaton, who brought out the best in Shrimpton. 'Bailey realised that by wearing Levis and jackboots, and clothes that militate against her sweet-briar appearance "the Shrimp" can belong to the contemporary scene,' he said.

'Miss Shrimpton's appeal is not so much in her baby-blue eyes, cleft underlip and cosy round cheeks but in the length of her extremities and the underwater manner in which she wields them.' Beaton was clearly smitten and so, too, was Bailey.

He remembers her as someone who was always on time, never threw a tantrum, appeared to have never-ending stamina and was impulsively generous. He recalls:

I don't think there has been anything like Jean, she was a kind of beauty of the century in a democratic way. She appealed to men, women . . . everybody. One of the things I loved about Jean was that she took modelling with a bit of dignity. Honestly, I don't think she cared if she did it or not, but with Jean you never had to re-shoot anything.

It's funny, though, that in terms of personal style she didn't have any. She just dressed in any old rags – most of the time she looked like a bag lady.

Bag lady or not, Shrimpton and Bailey were briefly engaged before she started going out with Terence Stamp. By 1966, however, her relationship with the actor, which fascinated the public, was on the rocks. She said:

We were so vain that we continued to dress ourselves up and go out to be looked at. I was so insecure that I was always fiddling in the bathroom or running to the ladies to check my appearance. It was pathetic. Here I was, at the height of my fame, behaving like this. I was just an accessory to this beautiful star and it was Terry's beauty that I was in love with – not the man himself. I was under a spell.

Shrimpton's modelling career continued until 1972, when she was 30. She made one movie, *Privilege*, which bombed. After her taste of stardom she ran an antiques shop and then took over the 300-year-old Abbey Hotel in Penzance. 'It's nice to be at the end of the world,' she told Bailey in 1999. She subsequently sold the hotel. And of her modelling career, she said: 'It was great fun becoming famous, but I got tired of it.'

THE DESIGNERS

Mary Quant

In her first column of the year for the *Sun*, celebrated woman's writer Jean Rook predicted that 1966 would be 'The Year of the Bosom'. 'Girls are back on the old standard – 37-22- and who notices the rest?', she told her readers. Meanwhile, designers in Paris predicted hemlines would be higher than ever – 'at least five inches above the knee bone'.

Think of the miniskirt, the defining fashion statement of the year, if not the decade, and you think of Mary Quant. Quite simply, she was the catalyst for the Sixties revolution in fashion, the hippest designer in the hippest city in the world. And the miniskirt was what made her famous.

Quant took the snobbery out of fashion and, in her own words, made it 'the great leveller'. In 1966 she was at the height of her fame and popularity. She was awarded the OBE and turned up for the ceremony at Buckingham Palace in a minskirt. In the same year, at the age of 32, she wrote her autobiography.

Yet Mary Quant was no overnight phenomenon. She opened her first boutique with her husband-to-be, Alexander Plunket-Greene, in 1955 and used to buy her material from Harrods because she didn't have to pay for it for a year.

Her boutique, Bazaar, was an instant success and soon attracted a celebrity crowd, the Beatles among them. But frustrated at the lack of creativity in the clothes she was selling she began designing them herself. Sparked by her innovative designs, Sixties fashion exploded into a riot of different colours, prints and fabrics and Quant was always at the forefront.

She explained her success in A.E. Hotchner's *Blown Away: The Rolling Stones and the Death of the Sixties*:

> I think I broke the stranglehold that Chanel, Dior and other designers had on fashion. I created styles at the working girl level. It was very gratifying to see that not only the mods wanted my clothes but so did the millionaires. They had everything else . . . but they didn't have any fun clothes. In the shops you found duchesses jostling with typists to buy the same dresses.
>
> Good designers know that to have any influence they must keep in step with public needs and that 'something in the air'. I just happened to start when that something in the air was coming to a boil. I just happened to fit in exactly with the teenage trend with pop records, coffee bars and jazz clubs.

By 1966 everyone wanted to wear her clothes because all the film stars and musicians did. When Beatle George Harrison married Patti Boyd in December 1966 they both got spliced in Quant creations. She also designed the costumes for *Georgy Girl*, an Oscar-nominated film which was released during the year.

Mary Quant – the catalyst for the revolution in Sixties fashion. *(Ted West/Getty Images)*

Her 'London look' meant simple lines, short or shorter skirts and bright colours, and the public couldn't get enough of it. And unlike most designers, who were much older than the models who wore their clothes, Quant was of the same generation as her clientele. She became synonymous with the bob haircut and the bold eye shadow that were all the rage. After David Bailey had photographed Twiggy and Jean Shrimpton in Quant clothes, he invariably turned the camera on the designer herself. 'I had a very strong idea of how I wanted to look. An innocent child look – that's what it was,' she said.

Quant's designs played with proportion, and she even put women into men's clothing by showing that men's shirts – slimmed down, elongated and worn with tights – could be fashionable. She was also responsible for hot pants, the slip dress, raincoats made out of PVC and the Lolita look.

By the end of the year she had turned her attention to cosmetics and her new range, not surprisingly, was a massive success. In fact, cosmetics rather than clothes eventually made her fortune. She recalls: 'At the time, cosmetics were stuck on three shades of eye shadow. Brushes were a foot long and lipstick was pink, red or orange. I wanted a collection you could carry around in a small handbag.'

Almost as famous as Mary Quant was Mary Quant's hair. The 'bob cut' or 'five point geometric cut' was created for her by Vidal Sassoon whose high-profile clientele included Jean Shrimpton and the American actress Mia Farrow, who had become engaged to Frank Sinatra in 1966.

Mary Quant continued to design long after the decade she helped to dress had ended, and she remains a household name in the world of fashion fifty years after opening her first boutique. She was bought out of her company in 2000 and now works as a freelance, spending time between her homes in Surrey and the south of France.

Yves Saint Laurent

Yves Saint Laurent was one of the brilliant young designers establishing his reputation in 1966. He had inherited Christian Dior's fashion house nine years earlier before going it alone. And in 1966 he opened his own chain of boutiques, called Rive Gauche, which soon expanded to over 150 shops worldwide.

YSL took his inspiration from art. His pop art dresses would be decorated with Mondrian paintings or even comic strips and later in the year he introduced masculine tailoring for the female market, starting with his smoking jacket for women. This was quickly followed by the knickerbocker suit and then culottes.

Barbara Hulanicki

In 1966, Barbara Hulanicki opened Biba in Kensington Church Street and it quickly became a way for life for fashion-conscious young Londoners. While some people sat in sofas in the window star-gazing, others rummaged in the gloom looking for a bargain gingham dress. There really was no boutique like it at the time.

The clothes were affordable and Hulanicki's tight, straight-fitting dresses extremely popular, but finding something was all part of the Biba experience. For starters, the clothes weren't on rails but on hat stands and the lighting was kept to a minimum with a chessboard floor and dark mahogany screens. And if the swirly wallpaper didn't give you a headache the thumping rock music from the big hi-fi unit would. They even had communal changing-rooms, unheard of in 1966. That was one phenomenon of the year which didn't catch on.

Barbara Hulanicki in her famous Kensington boutique Biba, complete with unisex changing rooms. *(Larry Ellis/Express/Getty Images)*

THE FASHIONS

Miniskirts

Nothing defined fashion in 1966 more than the miniskirt. Mary Quant will be for ever associated with bringing it to the mass market. But it was French designer André Courrèges who is credited with its invention – although in the mid-Sixties there was little sign of it becoming popular in Paris, let alone catching on in London and elsewhere.

All that changed in November 1965, when Jean Shrimpton, by now a model with global popularity, was asked to present the prizes at the Melbourne Cup race meeting, the biggest event in the Australian social calendar.

She was contracted to wear a dress made out of a synthetic material called Orlon, but her supplier didn't provide her with ready-made outfits. Instead, they gave her material and she came up with designs which she asked a dressmaker to turn into a dress. Unfortunately there was not enough material for Shrimpton's designs. Colin Rolf, who was the dressmaker, told her: 'Oh, it doesn't matter. Make them a bit shorter – no one's going to notice.' 'And that's how the mini was born,' said the Shrimp. She chose four outfits, all above the knee.

She turned up at Melbourne Park without stockings, hat or gloves. The organisers were shocked, the crowd bemused but the photographers couldn't get enough of her new look. Within hours, pictures of Shrimpton were on the front pages of nearly all the British newspapers. And when Jean Shrimpton wore something, it invariably attracted a following.

It was Quant who brought the design to the consumers, at prices they could afford. Shrimpton explained: 'Mary Quant rode in on the back of it, immediately making shorter skirts. Many people gave her credit for the new craze, but the truth was that the mini took off because Orlon had been stingy with the fabric.'

Anybody who had the legs to pull it off – and sometimes those who didn't – wore the mini. In New York the norm was 4–5in above the knee but in London anything less than 8in was considered positively staid.

Young people loved the mini, but it had mass market appeal. Its popularity even spawned the British Society for the Preservation of the Mini Skirt. In September they demonstrated outside Christian Dior because his new collection featured long dresses and coats. Protesters carried banners proclaiming 'Mini Skirts Forever' and 'Support The Mini'. At one time the society boasted 450 members.

It seemed women's skirt lengths were a barometer of contemporary attitudes and in 1966, when the Swinging Sixties were at their height, so were hemlines. By the end of the year the mini had become the micro-mini and Quant had also invented the maxi-coat, to keep those over-exposed legs warm, and panty hose.

Anything goes in 1966 – even the combination of miniskirts and fur coats. *(Copyright © popperfoto.com)*

Go-Go Boots

The fashion that four decades later was to spawn hundreds of websites dedicated to kinky boots was born in 1966.

Honor Blackman had first made go-go boots a fashion accessory. She wore them at ankle height when she played Cathy Gale in *The Avengers*. But by 1966 they had crept up to knee height and Nancy Sinatra lived out every man's fantasy when she wore a pair of white go-gos singing *These Boots Are Made For Walking*, which was a top-three chart hit in January.

Soon every woman who had the legs to get away with them was wearing go-go boots. Blackman even made a song in honour of them with her co-star, Patrick McNee, twenty-four years later.

4

THE MAN IN THE MAC

THE MAIN MAN

Harold Wilson was the man who shaped the Labour Party and the political mood in the Sixties. He helped to shape Mike Yarwood, too.

With his pipe and plastic mackintosh (the electorate knew little about his liking for cigars and well-aged cognac, for he burnished the common touch) he was a godsend for jobbing mimics everywhere.

Wilson was the small, owl-like man who cast a giant's shadow. He was the dominating figure in British politics for a dozen years, from when he first became Prime Minister in 1964 until his retirement from No. 10 in 1976. He won four of the five general elections he fought. And he was at the absolute peak of his powers in 1966.

The twists and eddies of his time in Downing Street, problems with trade unions, Rhodesia, Northern Ireland not to mention a little bother with France among others ('Events dear boy, events,' Harold Macmillan had called them) confounded his plans and determined that he would not go down as one of the nation's greatest statesmen. Whether he had it in him to achieve greatness, given a kinder wind, is a matter of considerable conjecture.

But this was still a remarkable politician. Intellectually formidable, Machiavellian, a show-off ringmaster who revelled in juggling the many class acts that surrounded him and in his brilliance at the dispatch box and in putting hecklers in their place, he could also be viewed as a man of fundamental decency, although one driven to the creation of a better society more through economic growth than social redistribution. Ultimately, there was failure. Strikes and a wobbly pound decided that. Throughout his many frustrations there were successes, too. His greatest political achievement, though, was to hold together his party in the midst of bitter internal wrangling.

When he died, following harrowing years of degenerative illness, he was not a rich man. The lucrative lecture tours would be a perk for later prime ministers. Some of his obituary notices were short of riches, too. There were many, while recognising his cleverness, who looked back on him as something of a political opportunist.

He had been born fifty years before the 1966 election, in the middle of the First World War, in a lower-middle-class home near Huddersfield. His father was an industrial chemist who worked for ICI, his mother a teacher.

His father, James Herbert, whom he would proudly take to Labour Party conferences, was made redundant in the post-war slump. This brought a sharp focus to the boy Harold's mind.

He attended Milnsbridge New Street Council School, where he won a scholarship to Royds Hall secondary school in Huddersfield. When his father found a job on the Wirral he was transferred to Wirral Grammar School, where he won a history scholarship to Jesus College, Oxford.

In his obituary of Wilson, in the *Guardian* of 25 May 1995, Geoffrey Goodman wrote:

> He wasn't typical. Unlike Denis Healey, from a roughly similar background in Yorkshire, Wilson did not dive headlong into Oxford politics or literary life.
>
> He was a swot. He spent his time almost exclusively on his studies – and did brilliantly. He won the Webb Medley economics prize as well as the Gladstone history prize. He gained an outstanding first-class honours degree and was elected to a junior research fellowship at University College, where he helped the master, Sir William Beveridge, in a study of unemployment and the trade cycle which had a clear influence on the great Beveridge Report.

After completing his degree Wilson stayed on as a lecturer. He joined the Civil Service at the outbreak of the Second World War and had a number of jobs – at the Ministry of Fuel and Power, the Ministry of Supply and the Cabinet Secretariat. In 1945, at the age of 29, he was awarded the OBE for his work behind the scenes during the war.

His career continued to follow a steep upward gradient. He stood, successfully, for the Ormskirk seat in the 1945 general election and was swiftly made Parliamentary Secretary to the Ministry of Works. He was promoted to Secretary for Overseas Trade in 1947 and six months later, at 31, became the youngest Cabinet minister for a century when he was made President of the Board of Trade. Shortly before Labour lost power in 1951 Wilson had resigned from the government, joining the left-wing Aneurin Bevan in protest against the NHS charges in Hugh Gaitskell's Budget. However, when Gaitskell became party leader in 1955 Wilson canvassed and voted for him, not for Bevan. Some in the party would never entirely trust him again.

Following the death of Gaitskell Wilson became leader of the party in 1963. In his book, *The Labour Party Since 1945*, Eric Shaw said: '[he] was distrusted as much for his guile and ambition as he was admired for his mental agility and adroitness.' Shaw continued:

> Wilson was, both by background and experience, drawn to meritocratic themes. But he was also searching for policies which could heal the divisions which had troubled the party for a decade, reaching a crescendo in the battles over Clause Four and nuclear weapons policy at the start of the decade. At the same time he wanted a message which could provide the party with a sharp campaigning edge.

Wilson portrayed Labour as the party of technological advance and scientific discovery. The Tories were painted as a bunch of amateurs and grouse-shooting aristocrats. Sir Alec Douglas-Home, who had only a frail grasp of economics and who once said he found it difficult to come to grips with the subject without using matchsticks, had difficulty competing. Wilson moved to No. 10 after the 1964 election having enthused voters with his famous speech on the 'white heat of technology' in the Labour leadership election. The election, though, was won by just five seats. Wilson's considerable parliamentary skills were seen at their sharpest as he held the government together for seventeen months with a majority over the Conservatives and Liberals that fluctuated between five and one. Inevitably, he went to the country again, in 1966. This time he won, convincingly, lost, to his surprise, in 1970, won twice more in 1974 and handed over to James Callaghan in 1976, when he was knighted.

He was made a life peer in 1983 and sat in the Upper House until his death twelve years later, though his later years were blighted by Alzheimer's Disease. Goodman, in his obituary, concluded:

> Lord Wilson of Rievaulx, as he came improbably to be called, will not go down as one of Britain's greatest Prime Ministers. But, increasingly, he will be seen as a far bigger political figure than contemporary sceptics have allowed, far more representative of that uniquely ambivalent mood of Britain in the 1960s and a far more rounded and caring, if unfulfilled, person.
>
> Harold Wilson, in my view, remains a remarkable man and a remarkable Prime Minister. He alone – other than [Clement] Attlee in 1945 – was capable of making Labour the 'natural party of government' and main-taining a unity within such a disparate and warring coalition of ideas and ambitions. He failed to rise to greatness because he failed in the critical period after the victory of 1966.

Ian Aitken was one of the leading political commentators of the period. Then the political editor of the *Guardian* – and now living in jovial retirement in leafy Highgate in North London – he says:

> In reality, Wilson was no more Machiavellian than other prime ministers. But he was probably more overtly so. Considering the awful problems he faced in 1966 he wasn't a bad prime minister.
>
> You have to remember that the party had been ripped apart by the Gaitskellites and the Bevanites and Wilson had a cabinet that was divided pretty well 50/50 between the two factions. They all not only hated each other but totally distrusted each other. Harold, of course, had been a Bevanite, and resigned, along with Bevan himself, from the 1951 government. But he was never regarded as a totally reliable Bevanite. He had the terrible job of holding the whole show together and stopping his Cabinet from tearing each other apart, and he largely succeeded. He was also right that there were many people who wanted to get rid of him as leader, though the only viable alternative at the leadership election had been the rather drunken figure of George Brown.

Aitken clearly has respect for both Wilson and Ted Heath, his main pro-tagonist. 'Wilson came to see me in hospital after I had had an eye operation. I said I thought Ted had fought a good, honest campaign in 1966. And he said, "What!!" He was absolutely outraged by the idea that Ted had been anything like honest. He was quite scornful of him and said Ted rolled over on his back like a spaniel whenever he received the slightest encouragement from Europe, particularly Paris, about entry into Europe. But I got to like Ted. We remained friends, exchanged Christmas cards and even had the occasional lunch.'

LABOUR BEFORE THE ELECTION

Wilson had been surprised by the narrowness of his victory in 1964. However, the steel debate, some setbacks in by-election results and an upswing in the polls for the Conservatives dissuaded him from calling a second election quickly. He also wanted time to establish the authority of his government and its leading personnel. He continued to attack the Conservatives for 'the thirteen wasted years', the 'Tory mess' and the fact that he inherited 'an £800 million trade deficit' when he came to power. But that deficit and Wilson's determination to defend sterling created problems for the government. Exchange controls were tightened, hire purchase repayment periods were cut, and so was public spending.

He resisted pressure from the left of the party, especially when it came to foreign policy. But he placated them with his decision to resist overtures from America, who wanted Britain to get involved with the war in Vietnam.

Double agent George Blake was sprung from Wormwood Scrubs prison in October and fled to the USSR, having served just five years of a forty-two-year term for spying. Blake was captured while serving in Korea and converted to Marxism during three years as a prisoner of war in Seoul. There were suggestions that he had been brainwashed, but he always maintained it was voluntary.

Sent to Berlin as a double agent in 1953, he betrayed the secrets of hundreds of MI6 agents to the Russians before he was exposed in 1959 and sentenced to 42 years in prison two years later. His jail term remains the longest tariff handed down by a British court. Newspapers at the time claimed it was a year for each of the agents he had double-crossed who were subsequently killed.

Two clues were found shortly after the escape: ten pairs of size 13 knitting needles and some flowers. The needles were used to reinforce the home-made ladder by which Blake made his escape and the flowers marked the escape point.

Aged 84, Blake still lives in Moscow on a KGB pension.

There was another overseas problem he could not ignore. In November 1965, Ian Smith made a unilateral declaration of independence in Rhodesia. Wilson ruled out the use of force but introduced economic sanctions, including an oil embargo. Any worries that Wilson could control the House of Commons, with his narrow majority, however, were soon dispelled and the Conservatives, for the most part, were kept on the back foot. It was in the Commons that Wilson was often seen at his best.

In their superb book about this time, *The British General Election of 1966*, the authors David Butler and Anthony King tell us: 'Mr Wilson had one other important item of political capital: his own reputation. It was essential to him that he not only be, but also appear to be, a master of political tactics. Partly it was a matter of *amour-propre* and of a long-standing sense that the Labour party valued him most for his political adroitness.

'But in the circumstances of the 1964 parliament his reputation was of more immediate value. It undoubtedly daunted the Conservatives, who felt they had no-one to match him. Fear of Wilson's tactics as well as the tactics themselves kept the Conservatives off balance; with another Labour leader, for example, they might not have been so apprehensive of a snap election.'

Not all Labour MPs and workers were happy with Wilson. A gap developed between government and party, something that today's critics of Tony Blair's style would do well to consider. Those NEC members who were not inside the government circle felt isolated. So did Transport House, the party's headquarters. And the success of the party's advertising campaign before the 1964 election persuaded the government to turn more to professional advisers. But there would be no quick election to increase Labour's majority. The by-election defeat at Leyton of his newly appointed foreign secretary, Patrick Gordon-Walker, and an upswing in popularity for the Conservatives, for whom Heath was now punching his weight instead of Douglas-Home, put paid to that. So did the protracted debate over steel nationalisation. But as the winter of 1965/6 dragged on it became increasingly clear that Wilson would go to the country again in the spring.

Wilson was personally popular with the voters and in January his party had held a good lead over the Tories in the opinion polls for four months. A positive by-election result in Hull hardened Wilson's mind towards a March election. On 28 February it was announced that the election would take place on 31 March. According to Aitken, a clever ploy by the government helped them to win the crucial Hull by-election. 'It must have been one of the biggest election bribes ever made,' he said. 'It came in the form of the Humber Bridge and it was provided by the Minister of Transport, Barbara Castle no less, and it still stands as a monument to her and that election. Labour won the seat by a handsome majority on the basis of that.

CONSERVATIVES BEFORE THE ELECTION

At the start of the decade the party and the country had been led by Harold Macmillan – the wily Supermac who told everyone that they had 'never had it so good'. He was followed by the thoroughly decent but hardly charismatic figure of Alec Douglas-Home. They could just as easily have been leaders at the start of the century. Now, with the Sixties in full swing, it was as if they belonged to a different aeon. Bowlers were being blown off and brollies turned inside out by the winds of change. Even politicians had to change with the times.

Douglas-Home's integrity had impressed everyone in the party. And, against all the odds, he had come close to winning the 1964 election. But there had always been a sense of the temporary about him.

Many viewed him as little more than a stand-in. He resigned as leader in July 1965. His successor would be one of Edward Heath, Reginald Maudling and Enoch Powell. In the July contest Heath received 150 votes, Maudling 133 and Powell 15. Heath did not have the necessary 15 per cent winning margin over his nearest rival but as Maudling and Powell withdrew a second ballot was not needed and Heath became the new leader of party.

Heath launched a major policy review, with immigration, trade union reform and the modernisation of the economy and social insurance high up on the agenda. But as Peter Joyce explained in his book, *UK General Elections 1832–2001*, it was not easy. 'Initially, Heath faced a number of difficulties. He found it hard to mount an effective challenge to Wilson's taunts that if

In a changing political landscape, Ted Heath's Conservative Party was still considered the party of the upper classes. *(Eamonn McCabe/Express/Getty Images)*

Conservative policies were so good why had they not been introduced during the thirteen years when they held office.' The Conservatives also had a problem with Rhodesia, and were split over the issue of an oil embargo following Ian Smith's unilateral declaration of independence.

Heath had become chairman of the Advisory Committee on Policy in 1964. He knew that the party would have to embark upon a programme of modernisation. Aware that Labour had stolen a march on modern business ideas and technology, as well as market research, he was anxious to bring in business and professional men as well as university teachers to provide fresh incentives.

A fresh document, 'Putting Britain Right Ahead', was produced. The party's commitment to Europe was reasserted. The relationship with trade unions was reassessed, with a call for more productivity bargaining.

Heath chose not to reset the party's entire philosophy. Instead, he decided upon a detailed examination of specific areas of policy. But there was a problem for Heath and the entire Conservative Party. While modernising, which included a streamlining of Central Office, there was a constant awareness that a new election could be called at any time and almost certainly within two years.

But the work went on. The party had used surveys before but now it employed them in a deeper and more sophisticated way. It did not like everything it heard. Many thought the Conservative Party was out of date and short of ideas. Others perceived that it was the party of the upper classes. It had neglected social issues. Many felt that if only the 1966 election had been called nine months later the party would have been thoroughly prepared. As it was, the results of the survey were still coming in when, with Heath's popularity faltering in the polls, Wilson decided to go the country.

LIBERALS BEFORE THE ELECTION

Led by Jo Grimond, the Liberal Party's manifesto was entitled *For All the People*. The party acknowledged that Labour would win the election and was eager to work with it, as it had been doing since 1964. In Scarborough, in 1965, Grimond declared that he would support the government where the two parties were in agreement, but would be prepared to trigger an election by voting against it if necessary.

Grimond's offer was based on the probability that Labour would lose its minuscule overall majority. But it never would, so the Liberals never held the balance of power, the bargaining muscle, that they had envisaged.

The party's familiar dilemma had once again been obvious at the 1964 election. They more than doubled their vote that year, jumping from one and a half million to over three million. And they won two more seats.

Liberal leader Jo Grimond. His party failed to hold the balance of power he'd imagined before the election campaign. *(Reg Speller/Fox Photos/Getty Images)*

Butler and King summed up the party's difficulties as it approached the 1966 election. 'The Liberals' most serious problem lay in sustaining morale and enthusiasm. The 1964 results had impressed outside observers but had left the party workers somewhat dispirited after the heady days of Orpington and West Derbyshire.

'The Liberal by-election victory at Roxburgh acted as a tonic but then came Mr Grimond's Liberal-Labour initiative and dissension both nationally and in the constituencies. In 1966, further depression was caused by reports that Mr Grimond was considering resignation. He had been leader now for nine years, was growing weary of incessant campaigning, and had been discouraged by the confused reception accorded his overtures to Labour.'

Grimond's willingness to work with Labour dismayed many potential Liberal voters and even split his MPs. There was support from the rising stars of the party, David Steel and Jeremy Thorpe, but fierce opposition from Peter Bessell and Emlyn Hooson. Party chairman Lord Byers also expressed his considerable doubts about any pact.

Hooson, the MP for Montgomery, spoke for many when he said: 'There is only one course open to the Liberal Party; that is to soldier on in complete independence of any arrangement with Conservative or Labour and to press for policies in which we believe.' The sceptics argued that Liberalism might be swallowed up by the Labour Party and that talk of an alliance would merely push potential voters in the direction of the two main parties. Some argued that any pact would have to be made with the Conservatives as soon as Labour lost its absolute majority.

THE CAMPAIGN

Ian Aitken remembers being on a plane with Ted Heath during the 1966 election campaign. 'It was a clapped out old DC3 and as we approached Glasgow there was a terrible clatter and crash and one of the windows dropped out close to where Ted was sitting. We were all a bit alarmed but landed safely enough. But the following morning the tabloids had a field day. They said Ted had almost been sucked out of the window because of the decompression – even though we had been flying at only 1,000 feet.'

But these were desperate times for journalists and voters alike because, as Butler and King pointed out in their book, the campaign was a great bore. 'It was a bore because there had been an election only seventeen months before and electioneering of a sort had hardly stopped for four years. It was a bore because campaign techniques that were new in 1959 had become, on the third time out, established rituals.'

The politicians were a little more interesting in 1966 than they had been. The first prime ministers of the decade, both Conservatives, had been Harold Macmillan and Sir Alec Douglas-Home. And by the middle of the Swinging Sixties they were beginning to look a little dated.

Harold Wilson had led the nation since 1964, infusing the electorate with fresh rhetoric. It was a Labour voice and it spoke of the 'white heat of the technological revolution'. Wilson succeeded because he caught the mood of the nation more quickly than his rivals.

But even Wilson and the rising young politicians from all three main parties could do little to make this election exciting. Like the result itself it was all a bit of a yawn. But the contest still generated great interest. The TV figures, like the actual voting numbers, were very high.

In contrast to all the excitement in 1964, Labour fought a quiet battle. Wilson came across as the professional, paternal figure, forever pointing out the failures of the Conservative governments between 1951 and 1964.

The Conservatives criticised Labour for their negative tone, for always going on about the past and never having anything constructive to say about the future. The integrity and wisdom of the Liberal leader, Jo Grimond, meanwhile, came over well in the much increased TV and press coverage of the day. But Liberals must have been dismayed that the death of Grimond's son towards the end of the campaign attracted more publicity than any of their arguments.

According to Peter Joyce, in *UK General Elections 1832–2001*, the issues that dominated the election were the state of the economy, entry into the European Economic Community and trade union reform.

> Wilson asserted that his government had accomplished more essential business in 500 days than the Conservatives had managed in 5,000. Wilson was an effective television performer and had used his talents to good effect since 1964 where his appearances had been highly polished and professional. The tone of the campaign in 1966 emphasised his reputation as a reliable, statesmanlike figure who would provide the nation with stability.
>
> The Conservative campaign devoted attention to Labour's alleged failings. It was argued that Labour had failed to deliver on its 1964 promise to end stop-go and to promote the steady expansion of the economy. The Liberal campaign was based on the premise (which was explicitly articulated) that Labour would win the election and that an increased force of Liberal MPs, supported by a large national vote, was needed to restrain Labour's future excesses and provide a 'brake on socialism'.

Get the picture? Even the negative, lowest-common-denominator tone of the 2005 election was occasionally more entertaining than this. There were moments, though, in 1966. Wilson, who usually sent his hecklers packing, came off second best when one of them hit him in the eye with a stink bomb. And on another occasion Quentin Hogg, who later became Lord Hailsham, brandished a walking stick in the faces of Labour hecklers. In many ways the Conservatives under Heath offered a radical alternative. They argued for trade union reform, the abandonment of agricultural subsidies and entry into the Common Market. But for every initiative there was the familiar taunt from the government: why didn't you carry out these policies in your thirteen wasted years?

More interesting, perhaps, than the campaign itself and the policies of the parties were the roles played in the election by TV and the press. As Martin Harrison pointed out in his essay in the Butler/King book, TV was playing an increasingly important part in elections.

For the first time the proportion of the population in homes equipped with television had risen to over 90 per cent, leaving television only fractionally short of the universal coverage of radio. Current affairs broadcasting continued its steady increase in output and importance. With the introduction of a largely revised structure of programmes, the BBC was now devoting about 10 per cent of its evening output to politics. In contrast to the heated controversy over its activities in 1964, broadcasting's place in the 1966 campaign was more generally accepted and understood.

For Labour, which still did not get the same support as the Conservatives among the newspapers, this was particularly important. Harrison went on to point out another trend that would become even more pronounced in subsequent elections.

Despite the expanded coverage the range of information remained surprisingly limited. The circle of politicians quoted in national bulletins actually shrank from sixty-one in 1964 to fifty-six. Mr Wilson, Mr Heath and Mr Grimond were in fact quoted more often than all others combined.

Indeed, if one measures time rather than quotations, Mr Wilson and Mr Heath alone had 53 per cent of all news time given to politicians of all parties. Both dominated their own party's coverage – Mr Wilson with 56 per cent of Labour time and Mr Heath with 70 per cent of Conservative time (largely because he took his party's press conferences). Thus broadcast news presented a strikingly 'presidentialised' campaign.

Despite the extended news coverage, however, the official election broadcast remained the focal point in the parties' planning. According to Colin Seymour-Ure, in a corresponding piece on the press coverage in the same book, 'newspaper men found the election rather tiresome'. The result of the election was never in serious doubt. And the pattern of circulation among the newspapers, as well as the ownership, was largely the same as it had been in 1964. It was still interesting to see how different newspapers showed their partisan colours. Seymour-Ure said:

A good example was one of the noisiest meetings of the campaign, Mr Wilson's visit on March 16 to the Birmingham Rag Market where Sir Alec Douglas-Home had been shouted down in 1964. The Communist *Daily Worker*'s headline read: 'Wilson Gets The Better Of Tory Hecklers'; the *Sketch*'s 'Hecklers Drown Wilson'.

The Tory *Sketch*'s story began 'Mr Wilson's big Birmingham rally ended in a shambles last night' and left no doubt that he had not coped with the hecklers very successfully. The *Daily Telegraph*'s headline was emphatic: 'Birmingham Youths Howl Wilson Down'. All the Labour papers made out that Mr Wilson had emerged victorious. So did the *Times* – one of the few papers without a firm partisan allegiance ('Mr Wilson giving as good as he took, finished by scoring a personal triumph in the way he stood up to the barrage of noise, chanting and cat calls') and the *Express* ('. . . within twenty minutes he had emerged as a cheeky chappy who, by sheer effrontery, had overcome an energetic and determined offensive against him'). The Labour papers were even more glowing: 'a superbly cool and talented theatrical performance' (*Guardian*).

In retrospect, Butler and King did not sound very excited by the 1966 election campaign. 'The great bulk of the participants and the observers of the 1966 campaign occupied their time very much as they had seventeen months before. Since they were not on tenterhooks about the result, they were often bored and felt that the whole process was wearisome and repetitious.'

Labour, especially compared with 1964, had fought a relatively subdued campaign. There were few gimmicks. 'You Know Labour Works' was their mantra. Nor did they ever waste an opportunity to harp back to the 'Thirteen Wasted Years' that had preceded their 1964 victory. In turn, Heath criticised Labour for the negativity of their tone. The Liberals, meanwhile, won much admiration for their policies and bathed in the publicity given them by the increased press and TV coverage.

THE RESULT

It was, as we have said, never in much doubt. Everyone expected a comfortable Labour victory and that is what happened. They gained an overall majority of ninety-seven, with a 75.8 per cent turnout. When Cheltenham became the first constituency to declare, at 10.04 p.m., there was a 2.9 swing to Labour.

This was before Peter Snow. The famous swingometer was a manually controlled prop in those days. But it still told the same story. This was followed by positive results from Salford and at 10.51 p.m., when it was announced that they had gained Exeter, there was no longer any doubt of a substantial Labour majority. Labour's vote was three-quarters of a million up on 1964 while the Conservatives' had fallen by over half a million. Labour's percentage margin, 47.9 per cent to 41.9, was the biggest for any winning party since Clement Attlee won for Labour in 1945.

Butler and King said in their book: 'More constituencies than ever before counted on the night. By 4 a.m. 460 results were in (in 1964 the figure had been 430 and in 1950 only 270). But the drama was continued on the Friday. It was not until just after noon that the 315th Labour victory was announced.

'Mr Heath, who had declined to make any statement the previous night, at 11.15 a.m. conceded defeat from his Albany flat. In the afternoon he held a press conference at Conservative headquarters. He handled the situation gracefully. He had no regrets. The Conservatives had fought the election in exactly the right way and would now offer vigorous constructive opposition; people had wanted to give Labour a longer period of trial.'

Butler and King also pointed out that there had been a remarkable uniformity in the swing to Labour. In almost half of the seats the swing had been within 1 per cent of the national average of 3.5 per cent. The Conservatives did not gain a single seat. The result confirmed that the voters had bought into Wilson's argument that the Labour Party had inherited some awful economic problems from the Conservatives and that they deserved a further period in office to put matters right. A Gallup poll before the election also revealed that, in personal

Not a Mac, but a suit. Harold Wilson, with his wife Mary, steps into No.10 for the first time. *(Fox Photos/Getty Images)*

terms, voters warmed more to Wilson than Heath. Almost twice as many (54 per cent) thought that Wilson had a 'strong forceful personality' compared with Heath's 28 per cent. Nearly four times as many people (15 per cent to 4 per cent) attributed a 'weak personality' to Heath rather than Wilson. The Liberals increased their vote and their number of seats. But their improvement was marginal and their leader, Joe Grimond, was left to reflect on a period in which he had made little real advance.

Labour were in control as completely as the Conservatives had been in 1959. But if the pragmatic Wilson gained confidence from his emphatic victory it would soon become dented by difficulties in the summer of 1966.

THE GOVERNMENT

The result of the 1966 election, with its comfortable victory margin for Labour, probably represented the apogee of the brilliant career of the little man from Huddersfield. Having led a government with a wafer-thin majority he had now been returned to Downing Street with a thumping mandate from the electorate. Just as Tony Blair was to do for Labour some thirty years later, the party was now established as the natural party of government, something that seemed unthinkable during the long years of Tory dominance.

Yet, for all the heady optimism and the brilliance of Wilson's team, the final analysis of the government that was formed in 1966 was that it failed. And it started failing pretty quickly. According to Ian Aitken, the government was beset by problems as soon as it took office.

'But the seamen's strike probably did more damage than anything else,' he said. Good things were ultimately done. But, overall, the government failed to achieve what it set out to do. And just as James Callaghan was to discover in 1979, when he went toe to toe with Margaret Thatcher, it was Labour's traditional supporters among the trade unions who would make life especially difficult.

In his book, *A Century of Labour*, Keith Laybourn concluded:

The tremendous victory which the Labour Party gained in the 1966 election confirmed it in its rising confidence that it was the party of power and government. It had secured for itself a sense of balance and authority. Yet this moment of confidence and euphoria was fleeting. By the end of the 1960s the mood had gone. What went wrong?

The economic problems of the late 1960s and the inability of the Labour government from 1966 to 1970 to deal with the trade unions confirmed to many voters that Labour had difficulty in running the economy effectively. Indeed, Wilson recognised this problem himself and in 1966 and 1967 decided that a fresh application for membership of the European Economic Community was in order. The French vetoed this move in May 1967 at a moment when relations between the government and the trade unions were declining further. Strikes, particularly the seamen's strike of May 1966, the wage freeze of 1966 and the devaluation of the pound in 1967, destroyed the trust between the Labour government and the trade unions.

Kevin McNamara, the man who opened the election door for Wilson by winning that famous Hull by-election at the beginning of the year, still feels a great deal of sympathy for that government. He said:

> **Prescription charges were cut by 1s because 13,000 NHS chemists were making too much profit – more than £859,000 at the last count.**

The problems that Wilson faced when he took over from Douglas-Home in 1964 are not always appreciated today. The prices and incomes policy was a difficult matter within the party – not the theory, but the practical application. There was the need to protect sterling and the increasing pressure from the United States government to intervene in Vietnam.

Then there was the aftermath of Suez and the need to withdraw, completely, from Singapore and Malaysia. And there was the constant problem of the smallest of majorities. He had real problems, major problems, the like of which Tony Blair hasn't had.

The majority was bigger in 1966 but the problems remained. This did not stop Wilson putting through a great number of important reforms in the Sixties. There was a major housing programme, rent control, a big push in comprehensive education as well reform in homosexual and capital punishment laws.

McNamara also praises Wilson for holding together a difficult government. 'He was surrounded by a government of intellectual giants. There was Healey and Jenkins, Crossman and Crosland, very formidable people. There was George Brown, too, who had not been to university but who had a terrific mind. And Peter Shore. In my forty years in parliament there has not been a team from either side to match the intellectual calibre and ideological conviction of that team. There were other bright minds who did not make it in the same way, like Brian Walden, as well as the young Shirley Williams and Roy Hattersley.' He continues:

And Wilson was outstanding in his own right, a brilliant economist who had made his name as a young man at the Board of Trade. He was outstanding at the dispatch box and a man who revelled in his own cleverness.

Above: Denis Healey. A cornerstone of Wilson's administration. *(Keystone/Getty Images)*

Left: Roy Jenkins advocated some forward-thinking policies during his time as Home Secretary, including a big reduction in the number of police forces. *(Central Press/Getty Images)*

Opposite: Anthony Crosland was one of Wilson's key cabinet colleagues. *(Ron Case/Keystone/Getty Images)*

The 1966 parliament was also the last time we had a major influx of trade union sponsored MPs, who came from the coal face and the factory floor. It was a very interesting time for me to be taking my first steps in parliament.

The major criticism I would make of that government is how it dealt with Northern Ireland. Wilson, in particular, had built up the hopes of the nationalist leadership. But the failure to face up to the problems and act on them resulted in the chaos that we saw in the riots that started in 1969.

Roy Jenkins said that he did not want to be dragged into the Irish bog. But the Irish bog started to drag them down and sucked up so much time and effort, as it has done with successive governments and, indeed, is still doing.

Under Wilson we sometimes felt like ambulance men. At best, we wanted to see a greater extension of social ownership. And a better concept of society. Tony Blair is more interested in managing capitalism better than those who have gone before.

Labour governed for four years and were convinced they would win another term when they went to the country again in 1970. The polls had been in their favour. But Heath was now beginning to thaw out in front of the voters. Here was not only a strong leader but, with his considerable achievements in the worlds of music and sailing, a substantial and rounded human being. He won a memorable victory that year. By the time Wilson returned to No. 10 in 1974 he was on his last political legs. Two years later he handed the keys for No. 10 to Callaghan and began his slide towards obscurity.

5

THE LOST GENERATION

For the people of Aberfan, the pain of what happened to their community on the morning of Friday 21 October 1966, when a slag heap slipped and engulfed the village school, will never go away. Most people born before 1960 remember what they were doing when they heard about the tragedy. Television and radio coverage turned it into a national disaster and more than 50,000 letters of condolence arrived in the village from all over the world.

Aberfan was one of the seminal moments of the Sixties and perhaps even the twentieth century itself, the shock felt a long way from the Welsh valleys. In the village itself, where 144 people lost their lives, the mental scars, both of those who survived and of those who were bereaved, will probably never heal.

In 2003, thirty-seven years after the tragedy, a study in the *British Journal of Psychiatry* revealed that as many as one in three survivors of Aberfan was still suffering from post-traumatic stress and that the children affected by the disaster were not always able to recover. The report claimed that many survivors suffered psychological effects for years afterwards, some for the rest of their lives. Yet only one social worker was assigned to the village in the twelve months after the tragedy.

The findings hardly came as a surprise to the people of Aberfan, not just the survivors but those who lost their loved ones on that misty Friday autumn morning when a torrent of colliery waste slid down from the 90-year-old tip which dominated the village and buried Pantglas Junior School, a hillside farmhouse and a row of houses in Moy Road close to the school. In total 116 children and 28 adults lost their lives. The school was engulfed at 9.15 a.m. and no one was found alive after 11 a.m.

Cliff Minett sent three of his children to the school that day, the last before the half-term holiday. Only his daughter, Gaynor Madgewick, survived. 'You never get over it, you just do your best to live with it,' he told the *Western Mail* in 2003.

Gaynor said: 'I'm not ashamed to say I've had counselling all my life and I still see a psychiatrist twice a year. I've been doing that since I was 16, but all the damage was done between 8 and 16.' She wrote a moving account of the tragedy when she was just 8 years old.

It wasn't until 1997, when hitherto withheld material about the tragedy became publicly available under the 30-year rule, that a true picture of the incompetence of both the Labour government and, in particular, the National Coal Board, emerged.

In 2000, Iain McLean, fellow in politics at Nuffield College and professor of politics in the University of Oxford, and Dr Martin Johnes, who lectures in sociology at Lancaster University, published *Aberfan: Government and Disasters*, a book which was partly funded by a grant from the Economic and Social Research Council. It was published on the thirty-fourth anniversary of the disaster. The *Guardian* said it revealed 'the full truth about Aberfan'.

Among their findings, they exposed the 'extremely insensitive' attitude of both the National Coal Board and the government towards the victims. 'The tragedy of Aberfan was exacerbated by the fact that the NCB was supposed to serve and be part of the community,' they wrote. Perhaps the best example of this was using proceeds from the charity disaster fund to help pay towards the removal of the tips which blighted other areas of the south Wales coalfield.

It wasn't until Labour were returned to power in 1997 that £150,000 was paid back to the disaster fund following intervention by the Welsh Secretary at the time, Ron Davies, who praised McLean for bringing the matter to his attention. 'It was a wrong perpetrated by a previous Labour government,' said Davies. 'I regarded it as an embarrassment. It was wrong which needed to be put right.'

The official inquiry, commissioned immediately after the disaster by Harold Wilson's government, published its findings in August 1967. The chairman, Sir Herbert Edmund Davies, laid the blame unequivocally with the National Coal Board and saved some of his most savage criticism for its chairman, Lord Robens.

He wrote: 'The Aberfan disaster is a terrifying tale of bungling ineptitude by many men charged with tasks for which they were totally unfitted, of failure to heed warnings and of total lack of direction from above. Not villains but decent men, led astray by foolishness or by ignorance or by both in combination, are responsible for what happened at Aberfan.'

Yet, no one lost their job, was demoted from office or prosecuted as a result of Aberfan. Even Lord Robens kept his post, despite his offer to resign. On the day of the tragedy, as men and women dug with their bare hands in a desperate search for survivors, Lord Robens was accepting a chancellorship from the University of Surrey. He refused to change his plans to visit Aberfan even when he heard about the unfolding disaster.

BEFORE THE TRAGEDY

Miners throughout South Wales, together with those elsewhere in Britain's coalfields, had long accepted the risks involved in their arduous job. The two biggest disasters in Welsh mining history occurred before the Second World War. In 1913, 439 miners were killed after an explosion and fireball at Sengenhydd, eight miles from Cardiff. It was the worst disaster in the history of British mining. In 1934, 266 perished at Gresford, near Wrexham, following another underground explosion.

Nationalisation of the industry between 1947 and 1951 should have been one of the finest achievements of the radical post-war Labour government and compensation, perhaps, for years of under-investment in Britain's coalfields and the exploitation of the miners who worked in them. But the accidents continued. In 1960, forty-five were killed at Six Bells, near Abertillery, and as recently as May 1965, seventeen months before Aberfan, an explosion at Clydach Vale claimed the lives of thirty-one miners.

Then there were the innumerable and less publicised smaller accidents which cost miners their lives on a regular basis. But, as McLean and Johnes point out, Aberfan was different. 'This time it was their children that were killed and, by implication, a part of the future was lost.'

The site of the tip had worried the villagers for years. In January 1964 a former mayoress, Gwyneth Williams, warned Merthyr Tydfil Borough Council's planning committee: 'We have had a lot of trouble from slurry causing flooding. If the tip moves it could threaten the whole school.'

Routine inspections of coal tips, such as the one from Merthyr Vale Colliery overlooking Aberfan, were carried out by the Coal Board but there were no regulations under the Mines and Quarries Act governing their safety. The Coal Board felt that they met their responsibilities but a lot depended on local circumstances. In the case of Aberfan, it seemed, the views of local people weren't listened to enough.

THE DISASTER

The worst disaster of its kind in Britain occurred just before 9.15 a.m. on the morning of Friday 21 October 1966.

Men working on top of the tip, which was over 800ft high and where colliery waste had been accumulating for thirty years, saw it suddenly fall away below them with a thunderous noise.

The torrent of black waste which began to move towards the village of Aberfan below had been set in flow by springs building up pressure in the fissured sandstone underlying the tip. The spring was well known by locals, but the Coal Board had denied all knowledge of it.

Two days of persistent, heavy rain had loosened the slag and when the pressure was released half a million tons of thick black liquid waste, about 45ft deep, began rumbling down the hillside, submerging everything in its path. The men on the top were powerless to prevent disaster. They had no emergency phone because the cable had been repeatedly stolen. The inquiry was later told that the disaster happened so quickly that an emergency call would not have been able to prevent loss of life. Although it was sunny on top of the tip, the village below was shrouded in fog with visibility down to around fifty yards in places.

First to be hit was a hillside farmhouse, where none of the occupants stood a chance. The owner and his wife were out shopping, but his mother-in-law and their two children became the first victims as the slide continued its path towards Pantglas Junior School.

In the village itself it seemed no one saw anything, but everyone was suddenly aware of the noise. When the slide came to rest it had engulfed an area half a mile across including the school and a row of eight houses in adjacent Moy Road.

Inside the school, it was the last day before half-term and the children had just finished singing 'All Things Bright and Beautiful' in assembly and were heading to their first classes of the morning. A total of 109 children were smothered to death in their classrooms, along with five teachers.

One of the most dramatic accounts of the immediate aftermath was given by 10-year-old Dylis Pope who, seconds before the school was engulfed, had been laughing with her classmates as their teacher took the register:

We heard a noise and we saw all this stuff flying about. The room seemed to be flying around. The desks were falling over and the children were shouting and screaming. We couldn't see anything but then the dust began to go away.

The teacher, Mr Williams, was also on the floor. His leg was caught but he managed to free himself and he smashed the window in the door with a stone. I climbed out through the hall and then out through the window. I opened the classroom window and some of the children came out that way. There were stones everywhere. The teacher got some of the children out and he told us to go home.

An even bigger loss of young life was averted because those pupils who were aged between five and seven were not due to start lessons until later in the morning. Others were saved because a bus bringing them to the school had been delayed. In total, ninety-nine families in Aberfan suffered a bereavement in the disaster.

Aberfan a few hours after its junior school had been engulfed by the slag heap. *(Terence Spencer/Time Life Pictures/Getty Images)*

THE RESCUE

Most villagers didn't see the tip engulf the school, but they all heard it. One likened the noise to 'an aeroplane dropping onto the school'. Within seconds of the slide coming to rest, mothers who had waved them off at the gates a few minutes earlier were running back towards the rubble to begin the frantic search for their children.

The agonies they must have endured during those desperate rescue attempts are still difficult to comprehend, even four decades later. Eye-witness accounts told of distressed women tearing away at the black waste with their bare hands because more sophisticated rescue equipment was still on its way.

One teacher was found with five children in her arms she was protecting. They died clutching each other for safety. As miners from local pits and the emergency services arrived the rescue operation began in earnest, but no one was pulled out alive after 11 a.m. – just 105 minutes after disaster struck.

Terrible as it was, the death toll could have been higher. Many children in the infants' classes were saved, along with their teachers. One woman, Pauline Evans, rescued children from a classroom which faced away from the tip by clambering through a tiny window. 'When I got inside there were about half a dozen children screaming in a room which had only half-collapsed. With the help of a nurse, I handed them through the window to safety.'

Those who were physically able to clamber through small windows found horrific sights of children crushed under their desks by the rubble or others, half-submerged in the waste, crying desperately for help. Some were rescued, but for most it was too late.

There was little hope, either, for those still trapped inside the houses in Moy Road which were destroyed. One 15-year-old victim was discovered in bed with the technical drawing he had been studying still in his hands. Almost everyone in Moy Road lost a relative or knew of someone who had been bereaved.

Thousands of villagers joined rescue workers in the agonising search for Aberfan survivors but no one was found alive two hours after the disaster happened. *(Jim Gray/Getty Images)*

As news of the disaster spread so Aberfan was besieged by hundreds of rescuers, the trained and also ordinary people from neighbouring communities whose first thought when they heard what had happened was to grab a shovel and head towards the village on foot, on the bus or in the car.

For most, it was a futile gesture. They simply got in the way of trained rescue teams, although by Friday afternoon literally hundreds of people were picking their way through the rubble, their grim task occasionally interrupted when silence was called for and another body was brought to the surface.

By the end of Friday around 1,000 miners, more than 100 soldiers and even a naval detachment of 200 sailors from HMS *Tiger* were engaged in the rescue operation, which continued into the night under the glare of giant arc lights. Local pits took men off their shifts to assist, firms diverted lorries and earth-moving equipment to the scene. Before its arrival human chains were formed to remove the rubble.

Some rescuers worked round the clock for three days apart from occasional breaks of no more than an hour and a half. Working shoulder to shoulder, they nibbled away at the mountain of black waste, shovelling the sludge along metal sheets to the waiting lorries. Weighed down by protective clothing and knee-deep in mud, the work was extremely difficult. But no one complained. They continued until, through sheer exhaustion, their bodies gave in, but there were always many others waiting to take their place.

The women who hours earlier had been first on the scene were now providing help of a different sort with food, drink and shelter for worn-out rescuers as they emerged from the rubble, their faces blackened except for the tear streaks. Two rescuers found the bodies of their own children, while another ran three miles from a local pit and was still digging in the sludge looking for his daughter nine hours later.

Meanwhile, on the tip itself, soldiers and miners put their own lives at risk as they stood watch in case of further slides. They would have been able to warn those involved in the rescue 500ft below, but there would have been little chance of finding safety themselves.

Bodies of the dead children were placed one to a pew in the village chapel. Only fathers were allowed to identify the corpses.

As the weekend began so more rescuers arrived, most of them volunteers. The local police cordoned off the village with two rows of barbed wire because ghoulish sightseers had ignored their calls to stay away. By now rescuers were working in twelve-hour shifts and, slowly but surely, despite more rain, they began to make inroads into the black waste.

By Sunday rescuers finally reached the wooden classroom floors. They were covered with pathetic mementoes of the children – an exercise book, coloured pencils and a tiny knitted glove.

Meanwhile, in the churches and chapels of the valley, the people prayed for strength to overcome their losses. As they did so, rescue workers slept away the exhaustion on the pews of churches being used as makeshift rescue centres.

Slowly but surely the landscape of Aberfan began to return to something which was more recognisable.

The disaster attracted media coverage from all around the world. Journalists who covered the story are still haunted by the images of what they saw. Among them was John Humphrys. These days he is the well-known anchorman for BBC Radio 4's *Today* programme. Back then he was a cub reporter on the *Merthyr Express* and was one of the first journalists on the scene.

In 2004 he made a series of programmes for BBC Wales on post-war Welsh history and is in no doubt as to the significance of Aberfan. 'It wasn't a key event, it was the key event. I think it made its mark on everyone who was remotely involved in it. For those of us who were there that day the mark is indelible,' he remarked.

'To watch those men digging in the muck that crushed their school in a desperate, and mostly futile, effort to save their own children was to witness human suffering on a different scale.

'I have seen many terrible disasters since then – too many – but nothing begins to compare with Aberfan. Other events pale into insignificance.'

A COMMUNITY IN MOURNING

It wasn't until 27 October, six days after the disaster, that the last body was recovered from the rubble. On the same day thousands of silent mourners from the south Wales valleys climbed the hills which separated them to attend the funerals of eighty-two victims of the tragedy.

Around 10,000 people gathered around the hillside cemetery overlooking the village as relatives, friends and official mourners filed through the silent streets to the simple fifteen-minute service. A convoy of hearses formed a shuttle service from the chapel where the coffins lay.

As each convoy made its way up the winding, rubble-strewn streets so groups of rescue workers and villagers stood, their heads bowed in silent tribute. Shops closed, many windows were draped in black and even pubs observed the official day of mourning. The only adult buried that day was Gwyneth Collins, who lived next door to the school. On either side of her lay a son.

Dominating the hillside was a giant cross made up of the wreaths received from all over the world.

On Saturday 29 October, eight days after the tragedy, two parents visited Aberfan. The *Western Mail* reported two days later: 'Never before had the Queen been so close to the people of Wales.'

The Lost Generation. *(Copyright © popperfoto.com)*

She arrived by train with the Duke of Edinburgh and there were the usual hand-shakes with local dignitaries. But this was like no other royal visit before or since. There was no flag-waving and no bunting. Nobody clapped and nobody cheered. All the Queen could do was offer sympathy and understanding when she met parents of some of the children who had died before thanking the rescue workers for their efforts, which were still continuing.

Aberfan was appreciative and warmed to the royal couple. They remained discreet and respectful until after the Queen had laid a wreath in the cemetery. But by the time they had begun to walk down Moy Road the crowds closed in and soon the Queen and the Duke were literally rubbing shoulders with the people of Aberfan. They spoke to those to whom they were introduced and also to those who happened to be standing there or waiting and watching from their doorsteps. There were policemen about, but they formed no security cordon. It

'Never before had the Queen been so close to the people of Wales.' The monarch and Prince Philip in Aberfan. *(Stan Meagher/Express/Getty Images)*

seemed that royal protocol had been left at the railway station. Now common courtesy took its place. The Queen, showing obvious signs of distress, was close to tears when she returned to the station after her two-hour visit as clearance work on the shattered school continued behind her.

Almost a year after Aberfan, the celebrated writer Laurie Lee visited the village. He found numerous tourists and souvenir-hunters and described the disaster fund as 'sprawling over the village like some great golden monster which no one can tame or put to good use'.

He heard 'a village chorus rising all day from the streets and pubs, a kind of compulsive recitation of tragedy, perpetually telling and re-telling the story . . . Most of them still live in a state of shock, in a village which remains an open wound.'

In *I Can't Stay Long*, which was published nine years after the disaster, Lee described in detail 'the village that lost its children':

> Fragments of the school itself still lie embedded in the rubbish – chunks of green-painted classroom wall. . . . Even more poignant relics lie in a corner of the buried playground piled haphazardly against a wall – some miniature desks and chairs, evocative as a dead child's clothes, infant-sized, still showing the shape of their bodies. Among the rubble there also lie crumpled song-books, sodden and smeared with slime, the words of some bed-time song still visible on the pages surrounded by drawings of sleeping elves.
>
> Across the road from the school, and facing up the mountain, stands a row of abandoned houses. This must once have been a trim little working-class terrace, staidly Victorian but specially Welsh, with lace-curtained windows, potted plants in the hall, and a piano in every parlour – until the wave of slag broke against it, smashed the doors and windows, and squeezed through the rooms like toothpaste.
>
> Something has been done to clear them, but not very much. They stand like broken and blackened teeth. Doors sag, windows gape, revealing the devastation within – a crushed piano, some half-smothered furniture. You can step in from the street and walk round the forsaken rooms which still emit an aura of suffocation and panic – floors scattered with letters, coat-hangers on the stairs, a jar of pickles on the kitchen table. The sense of catastrophe and desertion, resembling the choked ruins of Pompeii, hangs in the air like volcanic dust.

On the children who had survived the tragedy, Lee wrote: 'Prettily dressed and beribboned, riding expensive pedal-cars and bicycles, they are an elite, the aristocrats of survival, their lives nervously guarded and also coveted by those who mourn. By luck, chance, and by no choice of their own, they are part of the unhealed scar-tissue of Aberfan.'

Lee then went to the local pub and met the father of one of the young victims, who told him:

> Of course, we could have lost the boy too. He was on his way up Moy Road when he saw the houses falling towards him. He ran off home and I couldn't get a word out of him for months. He had to go to the psychiatrist. . . . Just wouldn't talk about it, and wouldn't mention his sister, either. And the two of them worshipped each other. They was always together; slept in the same room, holding hands. He used to hide when we went to the grave.
>
> Then one night – about four months later it was – we was round at our brother's place. The boy went outside to the lavatory and I heard him call, 'Dad!' 'Ay, what is it, boy?' I said. 'Come out here!' he said. 'Sure,' I said, 'What's the matter?' It was a beautiful frosty night. He said, 'Look at that star up there – that's our Sandie, Dad.' 'Sure,' I said, 'that's our little Sandie.'
>
> The boy's all right now, and I'm going to see he's all right. . . . And I'll make damn sure he never goes down the pit. He's not going to grow up daft like me.

THE INQUIRY

Within hours the distress suffered both by families of the victims and people in the village and beyond had turned to anger. Their ire was soon being directed at the National Coal Board and, to a lesser extent, Harold Wilson's Labour government.

The grief of the bereaved was mingled with a strong belief that the disaster could have been averted. Local people had warned for years that the tip might collapse at any moment yet no action had been taken.

With indecent haste it seemed, the Coal Board had announced within hours that the slippage had been caused by the recent heavy rainfalls. Yet how could they have come up with a theory so quickly?

The official inquest took place five days later and the mood was one of anger. As the recorder gave the cause of death as accidental, one distraught father shouted: 'No, they were murdered by the National Coal Board.'

It wasn't only the villagers who were demanding answers. Parliament and the rest of the country wanted the truth to be uncovered. The government was worried that newspaper and television coverage might influence the outcome of the inquiry and six days after the tragedy they imposed a blackout, effectively banning media organisations from speculating as to the causes of the disaster. This was an unprecedented move. In effect, the government now considered it *sub judice* to make any comment on how the disaster might have happened, outside those in the official inquiry. The Attorney-General warned that anyone who disregarded the instruction was liable to be charged with contempt of court and referred to the High Court for possible criminal proceedings.

But there was widespread support in the community when the government announced two days after the tragedy that a Welsh-speaking judge, Lord Justice Edmund Davies, would head the inquiry. A local man who had gone to school in nearby Mountain Ash, Lord Justice Davies was an expert on mining law. He knew the area well and he knew mining people and their families.

On the same day the Coal Board confirmed a crash programme of inspections of 500 tips in south Wales. More than 200 of them were reported to be in a dangerous condition.

Lord Justice Davies paid his first visit to the disaster area on 24 October. Although no villagers were allowed to accompany him on his tour, one victim's father broke the police cordon to confront him in Moy Road. 'Don't let strangers pull wool over your eyes about the facts behind the disaster,' he told him.

The judge promised no whitewash. 'If blame is found, blame will be cast,' he said. 'And if nobody is to blame then that, too, will be stated quite clearly.'

The judge was given full powers to subpoena attendance and call for documents. The tribunal began their deliberations at Merthyr College of Further Education and then, after Christmas, they resumed at a college in Cardiff. They sat for seventy-six days, making it the longest-running inquiry of its type in Britain at the time.

Lord Justice Davies was true to his word that no stone would be left unturned in the search for the truth about Aberfan. In all 136 witnesses, ranging from schoolboys to university professors, were called. More than 300 exhibits were examined and more than 2,500,000 words were heard. Evidence was taken on everything from local mining history to the geological conditions in south Wales.

It emerged again that local people had been concerned about the condition of the tip for years. Lord Robens' theory in the immediate aftermath of the disaster that the spring underneath the tip had caused the slide was quickly discredited. So, too, were the Coal Board for the complete absence of any coherent policy on tips and tipping.

The inquiry was nearing its completion when Lord Robens made a dramatic appearance to give evidence and admit that the Coal Board had, after all, been at fault. Had his admission been made at the beginning of the inquiry then the tribunal's work would have taken days rather than months. Lord Robens offered his resignation, but the Coal Board refused to accept it. The tribunal members retired on 28 April 1967 to consider their verdict and just over three months later, on 3 August, their findings were published.

Blame was laid firmly at the door of the Coal Board although the report was at pains to refute charges of outright villainy against certain individuals. 'Miners devote no more time to rubbish tips than householders do to dustbins,' the report said.

'The Aberfan disaster is a terrifying tale of bungling ineptitude by many men charged with tasks for which they were totally unfitted, of failure to heed clear warnings, and of total lack of direction from above.'

It emerged that as recently as 1963 there had been a substantial slide of the tip which caved in on 21 October 1966. Yet still the Coal Board chose to ignore it. That slide was not even recorded in their files. 'For nearly three years the event presented a vivid warning of the terrible dangers which loomed ahead. But it was a warning no one in authority ever heeded,' the report added.

'Blame for the disaster rests upon the National Coal Board. This is shared, though in varying degrees, among the NCB headquarters, the South West Divisional Board and certain individuals. The legal liability of the NCB to pay compensation for the personal injuries, fatal or otherwise, and damage to property is incontestable and uncontested.'

Lord Justice Davies concluded that the tribunal had little option but to accept Coal Board assurances that tipping procedures were now under control. The report singled out nine NCB employees for particular criticism but made it clear that this was a story 'not of wickedness, but of ignorance, ineptitude and a failure of communications'. No one faced criminal proceedings, but the nine individuals had Aberfan on their consciences for the rest of their lives.

Things had to change, and slowly they did. It was considered impractical to bury coal waste underground, which was done in Europe. Tips were left in the control of the Coal Board but in future they were treated as potentially dangerous structures subject to regular inspection. Although the Aberfan tip was declared safe after the slide, the government bowed to local pressure and ordered it to be removed in 1968.

The tragedy led to the Mines and Quarries (Tips) Act in 1969, which charged quarry owners with the design, supervision and inspection of tips.

THE AFTERMATH

The human response to the tragedy, both from the people of Wales and those living farther afield, was unprecedented.

As well as the many people who travelled from across Britain to help with the rescue operation, thousands sent donations to the appeal set up in the aftermath of the disaster by the Mayor of Merthyr. Many of the donations came from children who had raided the contents of their piggy banks or who sent their pocket money. By the Wednesday after the disaster the fund had swollen to £30,000 while an appeal launched by Princess Margaret was answered with donations of 5,000 toys.

Over 50,000 messages of sympathy arrived from all over the world and the Mayor of Bournemouth offered practical assistance in the form of free seaside holidays for children and parents affected by the disaster.

The loss of so many young lives and the suspicion that this was the human cost of years of cheap coal led to a widespread feeling that something, however small, had to be done.

The disaster fund finally closed five months later, in January 1967. A total of £1.75 million had been raised. Over 90,000 contributions had been received. At today's values the Aberfan appeal would have raised in the region of £17.5 million.

But from the outset the fund faced problems, not least because of the disquiet among villagers that there wasn't enough representation from the people of Aberfan itself on the committee appointed by Merthyr Borough Council to decide how the money would be spent.

Some donors wanted the entire fund to go to bereaved families while others felt it should benefit the wider community. There was little support for a proposal that some of the proceeds might be spent on removing other tips, but when neither the Coal Board nor the government admitted full financial responsibility the fund ended up paying £150,000 for the removal of the remaining tips in the Aberfan area. Thirty years later that money was finally refunded, but it remains one of the biggest scandals in the history of post war Labour governments. Even then, not a single penny was made in interest payments.

The fund was finally put on a proper legal footing but the disputes, almost inevitably, continued.

But a total of £812,000 was paid to 712 villagers, including £5,000 to each of the bereaved families. Around £450,000 was spent on a new community hall, swimming pool and play area, which was opened by the Queen seven years after the disaster.

Parents of children who died received £500 from the Coal Board, but had to prove that they were 'close' to their children before any payment for emotional suffering was made. It was a year before the ruined school and houses were removed as wrangling over liability continued.

Iain McLean believes that papers on the tragedy released in 1997 under the thirty-year rule simply prove how insensitive both the Coal Board and government were to the victims. He said: 'They were treated as troublemakers and officials had no concept of the trauma that these people suffered.'

The terrible events of 21 October 1966 still cast a shadow over Aberfan four decades later. This is a tragedy which will never be forgotten.

The village itself has changed little. The main A470 road from Cardiff to Merthyr runs above Aberfan right through the path of the slide. The Merthyr Vale Colliery closed in 1990 and landscaping of the site means there are few reminders that one of the busiest pits in the South Wales coalfield once stood there.

The site of Pantglas Junior School was eventually turned into a memorial garden which was refurbished a few years ago, while a community centre now stands on the site of the houses which were destroyed in the slide.

Thousands of tons of spoil from the tips was used to create a flood plain on which a sports field was built four years after the disaster. But Aberfan was back in the headlines in 1998 when around a hundred families living opposite the field had to be housed in temporary accommodation after floodwater swamped their homes, causing damage estimated at £1 million.

The local council and Coal Authority conceded that they had caused the flooding by raising the level of the land, but a judge ruled that they were not liable in law. Instead, in 2004 thirty-one families demanded compensation from the Coal Authority and Merthyr Borough Council.

The village chapel, which acted as a temporary mortuary in 1966, has been replaced although Aberfan's victims are remembered in a smart stone tablet. About half of the victims are buried in the hillside cemetery. On the entrance to the memorial garden is a simple but heartfelt inscription: 'To those we love and miss so very much.'

The physical reminders have mostly gone, but for survivors and the bereaved the emotional scars remain. Survivor guilt is a recognised condition these days and grief counselling would be offered to the bereaved were a similar tragedy to occur today. But in 1966 this was not the case. The men of Aberfan were expected to bear grief 'like a man'. Tears were a sign of weakness, not courage.

October is always the worst month of the year for retired staff nurse Sheila Lewis. The scars of bereavement will never go away but it is at this time of year

The Memorial Garden at Aberfan was built with the funds raised by a disaster appeal. *(Photo by Ken Gardner/TopFoto.co.uk)*

that the pain grows in intensity, an experience undimmed by the passing of four decades. It is something she feels will be with her for the rest of her life.

> There is an emotional clock inside my head and it starts ticking in September and doesn't stop until after the anniversary of the disaster. It makes sleeping very difficult, until the beat finally goes away.
>
> It's not unusual, so the doctors tell me. They have patients who went through terrible times in the Second World War and they have the same kind of feeling at a certain time each year.
>
> Most of the time I cope reasonably well. I'm pretty positive about life but it gets very difficult during this period. It's something I have learned to get through but it doesn't really get any easier.

Mrs Lewis's daughter, Sharron, was just 9 when she died in the disaster.

> The first I knew about the collapse of the school was when my other daughter, Patricia, returned home early. She didn't have her coat. She said she was sorry but that in all the confusion she had no choice but to leave it behind.
>
> I didn't know how bad it was until I went down there and turned the corner and saw what had happened and the commotion. I knew then that it might not come to a good end. I just hoped and hoped that somehow Sharron had escaped. But then, eventually, the devastating news came through.
>
> The first feeling I had was one of guilt. Why didn't I send Sharron to the Catholic school down the road instead? Again, I'm told this is a common response. Then came the anger as you cast around for others to blame. And of course that wasn't very hard because the National Coal Board were clearly to blame. That all came out when they held an inquiry.

Sheila had a disturbing dream early in 1966, months before the disaster. 'I dreamt that I was walking along a bridge with Sharron when suddenly it opened and she lost her footing and fell into the water.

'Then, after I woke up, I could hear her crying out for me. I told my husband about it and he told me I shouldn't make anything of it, but now I wonder.

'My one comforting thought is the belief that she didn't suffer at all. But I don't know that for a fact. It's a hope more than anything else.'

For a couple of years the grief-stricken mothers would meet. Pictures were exchanged and there was crying and laughter. 'You have to remember that this is a very small community. We supported each other. We still get together for anniversary services, when a number of churches combine. I don't go around crying all the time. But October is the toughest time of all.'

Nor was Sharron's death the only tragedy to strike the Lewis family. In 1992 her only son, Gwyn, recently married and the father of a seven-month-old daughter, was killed in a car crash. 'He was driving back from Lincoln at the time. It was so sad that it happened at that point in his life.'

Gaynor Madgewick, who lost a brother and sister in the tragedy, is still upset at the lack of support which was made available to the survivors. 'I feel very bitter that we never had conversations about this. I think it has ruined our lives.

'I have never settled down. I have moved house about fifteen times because I can't stay in one place for long. I know that I have over-protected my children. I have run their lives for them. I go to extreme lengths to make sure I protect and care for them. I've had counselling all my life since I was 16 but the damage was done between 8 and 16.'

Many survivors and relatives have moved away, but Gaynor's father, Cliff Minett, who is chairman of the Aberfan Disaster Fund, still lives in the village in a house which overlooks the cemetery. 'What we saw on that day had a terrible effect and the stress for some people must be terrible. I kept working. I think if I had stopped and thought about what I saw and went through on that day I would be in a terrible state. I did think of moving away but what's the point? It goes with you.'

One of the hundreds of rescuers, Enos Sims, is reminded of what happened each time he hears a news bulletin or reads a report of a tragedy elsewhere. 'Every time we hear about an earthquake our thoughts go out to those people and the rescuers because it is a very traumatic experience.

'It was a very sad place to be at one time, but as the years go on I believe something good will come out of it for the village.'

The world must hope that one day 'something good' will emerge. For now, a full forty years after the tragedy, Aberfan is still struggling to forget the day 'their mountain moved'.

6

FLOATING BUTTERFLIES AND OTHER STARS

Away from the World Cup, the sporting year of 1966 was dominated by the second showdown between world heavyweight boxing champion Muhammad Ali (formerly Cassius Clay) and Britain's great hope, Henry Cooper.

Three years earlier, 'Enry's 'Ammer – his left hook – had knocked down Ali in the fourth round in front of 55,000 fans at Wembley Stadium, but Ali, who had been granted precious extra recovery time between rounds while his split glove was examined by the referee, produced a ferocious onslaught in the fifth round and the fight was stopped in the sixth as Cooper wilted under a ruthless barrage.

When they met again in front of a 43,000 full house at Arsenal FC's Highbury Stadium in May 1966 Cooper was giving away eight years to his opponent and few gave him much of a chance. They were right to be pessimistic.

Mickey Duff co-promoted the fight with Jarvis Astaire and Harry Levene. 'It was, without doubt, the biggest fight ever staged in England,' remembered Duff. 'A British heavyweight was fighting on home soil for the championship of the world and, because of the knockdown in their first fight, people thought Cooper had a chance.'

Astaire wanted the fight to be shown on closed-circuit television and had thirty-two cinemas throughout the country willing to pay for the pictures. The BBC and ITV jointly appealed to the Postmaster General, Anthony Wedgwood, Benn, that the fight was of massive public interest and should be made available to all. Astaire and the rival broadcasters were summoned to the minister's London home one Sunday morning for a showdown. Amazingly, the arch-socialist Benn came down on the side of free enterprise. BBC and ITV would pay £32,000 for a recording of the fight and Astaire ended up clearing £100,000.

'There was one other problem I had to resolve,' recalled Astaire. 'The money Cooper wanted. His manager, Jim Wicks, was very obstinate and was holding out for £30,000 rather than a percentage of the takings. But, with the help of Mickey Duff, I persuaded him to accept a percentage deal which, in the end, earned Cooper £43,000.

Stage set. A full house of 43,000 fight fans packed into Highbury for the second Ali–Cooper fight. *(Harry Todd/Fox Photos/Getty Images)*

'Ali, of course, got a lot more. We guaranteed him $250,000 and he ended up receiving $560,000. You can multiply those amounts by eleven to get some idea of how much this would have been in today's terms.'

Cooper fought bravely, as everyone knew he would, and tried to nail his opponent with that trademark left hook. But Ali, who hadn't even visited the stadium prior to the fight (the weigh-in was held at Leicester Square) was too quick on his feet and too quick with the jab.

Two right-hand punches to the head opened up a deep gash above Cooper's left eye and the fight was stopped midway through the sixth round. 'In the end Cooper wasn't so much bleeding as leaking blood, slashed to ribbons above his eyes,' remembered Astaire.

While Cooper was taken to hospital to have twelve stitches inserted into a cut he claimed was the worst he had ever received, the speculation at ringside was that it been caused by a head-butt. Jim Wicks was convinced that Ali had used

Boxing fans queued in Leicester Square to catch a glimpse of Ali at the weigh-in for his second fight against Henry Cooper. *(Evening Standard/Getty Images)*

illegal means and called for him to be disqualified. But as the thousands of fans watching Astaire's closed-circuit coverage all over the country knew, the champion's blows were legitimate ones.

Ali was left unmarked apart from some swelling below his left eye. 'I hate to spill blood,' he told Cooper in the dressing room afterwards. 'It's against my religion.'

Ali was a sporting icon in 1966, although it could be argued that he was still to make the worldwide impact which came during the early Seventies with those memorable fights against George Foreman and Joe Frazier. And as he struggled to convince the authorities back home in the US that he shouldn't be drafted for army service in Vietnam, he made more successful visits to Europe during a hectic schedule which included five comfortable title defences between March and November in 1966.

On the attack. Henry Cooper is forced onto the defensive by Muhammad Ali.
(*Keystone/Getty Images*)

In August, he easily knocked out England's Brian London, appropriately enough in London, in the third round. Astaire refused to promote the fight because he feared a total mismatch. Again his judgement proved sound. A month later, Ali stopped Karl Mildenberger, the first German challenger for the heavyweight title since Max Schmeling, in the twelfth round of their contest in Frankfurt.

Duff co-promoted the Mildenberger fight with Astaire and remembers fondly an incident which took place outside the ring.

'Britain's Teddy Waltham refereed the fight and did an excellent job. The next morning I saw Teddy and he was as white as a sheet. We had paid him £1,000 in cash right after the fight. He'd lost it all.

'We got on the plane and I was telling Jarvis what had happened when I felt a tap on my shoulder. It was Ali and he asked, "Is that the guy who refereed my

The promoter. Mickey Duff, third from left, staged several Ali promotions in Europe. *(Allsport Hulton Archive/Getty Images)*

fight?" I said, "Yeah." Ali just shook his head and said, "That's a shame, he worked so hard." Anyway, when we got off the plane in London I saw Teddy and he was looking quite happy. I said, "You look like you've found your money." And he told me "Not exactly, but someone must have told Ali because he just gave me a thousand pounds."

'That was Ali. He'd asked someone how much a thousand pounds was in American money, went into his own pocket, and gave it to Waltham.'

Ali made another successful title defence in November, when he pummelled Cleveland Williams into defeat after knocking him down four times in the first round. One journalist whom Ali respected more than most at that time was ABC Television's Howard Cosell. He reckoned this was Ali's finest ever performance. A crowd of over 35,000, the largest attendance for an indoor boxing promotion, saw the Williams fight in Houston, Texas.

'That night he was the most devastating fighter who ever lived,' Cosell recalled. 'He was bold and young and strong and skilled, just coming into his prime as a fighter.'

Astaire, meanwhile, discovered that when it came to promoting the fights, no one could do the job better than Ali himself. 'Ali was a genius, an absolute joy. He had such a natural instinct for the job that you just let him get on with it and the ticket sales would follow.'

Astaire also saw at first hand the man's incredible largesse. 'When I was in Frankfurt when he was fighting Mildenberger, Ali was wearing a fabulous watch with a dial surrounded by diamonds, which I said I liked very much. That was it, he wanted to buy me one and he marched me across to the jewellers in the hotel lobby. I wouldn't accept the gift and he seemed quite put out.'

Ali never forgot Astaire, either. Five years later Astaire borrowed £4,000 from Ali to buy his wife Phyllis a watch when Ali was fighting in Switzerland. 'A week later I saw him at the Royal Lancaster Hotel and wanted to give the money back, but he wouldn't take it. It was around £4,000. He reminded me of the time he had tried and failed to buy me a watch in Frankfurt. It was clear to me it made him happy to be generous.'

In 1967, as he still refused the draft, Ali lost his US boxing license and didn't win it back until 1970.

If the Ali-Cooper fight was the biggest story in boxing, the saddest was the suicide in May of the former world middleweight champion, Randolph Turpin, at the age of 37. Turpin took his own life in the flat above his wife's café in Leamington Spa, Warwickshire.

Turpin was one of the finest middleweights Britain ever produced and had made his fortune by the age of 24 after winning the world title by out-pointing the great Sugar Ray Robinson in London in 1951. It was Robinson's first defeat in 133 bouts and Britain had their first black world champion.

A crowd of 61,370 paid £277,400 (a record at the time for a non-heavyweight fight) to see the re-match at the New York Polo Grounds just sixty-four days later, when Robinson won back his title with a sensational tenth round stoppage.

Turpin won the British title at light-heavyweight on two occasions before retiring in 1958, but by then most of his £250,000 had been squandered on reckless gestures such as the purchase of a castle in north Wales. By the end, Turpin was forced to earn a crust by boxing in fairground booths and on unlicensed promotions. He even briefly tried wrestling.

The public turned their back on him, but they never totally forgot the fighter who had once beaten the great Sugar Ray Robinson.

Britain did have its first world champion at flyweight since 1950 when Scotland's Walter McGowan beat Italian Salvatore Burruni over fifteen rounds at Wembley in June. McGowan lost his title to Thailand's Chartchai Chionoi later in the year, when the referee stopped the fight. He made an unsuccessful bid to regain it from the Thai boxer in 1967 and eventually moved up a weight division before retiring in 1969.

Former world champion Randolph Turpin died penniless in the flat above his wife's café. (*Chris Ware/Keystone/Getty Images*)

FOOTBALL

The Beatles weren't the only thing which were giving Liverpudlians a spring in their step. The city's two football teams dominated the domestic game in 1966. Liverpool won the Football League championship for the second time in three years under the legendary Bill Shankly, and Everton came from 2–0 down to beat Sheffield Wednesday 3-2 in one of the great FA Cup finals at Wembley.

Forty years later, in an era when professional clubs operate with huge staffs and managers carefully rotate their players, it is hard to imagine any club going through a month using just fourteen players, let alone an entire campaign. But that was the number Shankly employed throughout the whole season, and two of the players only appeared in a handful of games.

Propelled by 30-goal Roger Hunt, who was to maintain his league form in the World Cup finals later in the year, and strengthened at the back by the arrival of that no-nonsense defender Tommy Smith, Liverpool reached the top of the first division in November and were never headed again. They clinched the title with three games to go.

For club and country. Roger Hunt's goals propelled Liverpool to the league title and helped establish him in England's World Cup-winning team. (PA/EMPICS)

Skipper Ron Yeats still remembers fondly the inspirational Shankly. Surely no manager in the history of the English game moulded a side so strongly in his own image. It was taken as read that every member of a Shankly team gave every last ounce for the cause. As someone brought up in the working-class traditions of the game, the Koppites regarded him as one of their own. During that season he regularly joined them on the famous terrace to gauge the mood of the club's fanatical supporters.

'He made any player feel like a great player,' remembered Yeats. 'Even when we lost that season the boss would prove that it was all a mistake – the winning goal was offside, one of our blokes was fouled – that sort of thing.

Number one. Liverpool's great manager Bill Shankly.
(Coyright © popperfoto.com)

The champions. League winners Liverpool took over at the top in November and stayed there for the rest of the 1965–66 season. *(Central Press/Getty Images)*

'There were no non-triers in that team. He wouldn't tolerate any lax attitudes, no matter who you were. We didn't have any stars really, everyone was treated the same.'

Shankly had his humorous side as well, as Yeats remembers:

After we had just won the title but still had a few games to play out the season, he said to [goalkeeper] Tommy Lawrence: 'Wouldn't it be great if we could put a deckchair in the middle of the goal, you sitting in it, cigar in your mouth, and when the ball comes you get out of your deckchair and catch it and say, "It's a lovely day to play football, isn't it?"

Leeds United finished second on the same number of points as Burnley. Manchester United, who began the season with fifteen internationals on their staff, were expected to give Liverpool their stiffest challenge. In the end they finished ten points behind in fourth place.

There was to be no double for Liverpool, however. Over 134,000 watched them beat Celtic in a two-legged semi-final but in the European Cup Winners' Cup final at Hampden Park they were beaten 2–1 by Borussia Dortmund, Hunt's second-half goal having taken the tie into extra time.

Across at Stanley Park there were reasons for celebration as well. Everton enjoyed their first FA Cup final victory for thirty-three years and, as invariably seemed to happen in those days, the Wembley showpiece against Sheffield Wednesday threw up an unlikely hero.

Mike Trebilcock had only joined the club a few months earlier. He had demonstrated his potential with twenty-seven goals in seventy-one games for Plymouth Argyle in the old Second Division and returned from a trip to the cinema just before Christmas 1965 to find an Argyle director waiting on his doorstep to tell him that Everton wanted to sign him for £30,000.

Trebilcock made his debut in a 2–2 draw against Spurs on New Year's Day, but he had played just six more league games when Everton manager Harry Catterick chose him ahead of the more established forward, Fred Pickering, to face Wednesday in the cup final. Catterick felt his predatory instincts in and around the box would cause Wednesday more problems.

'Ahead of the cup final I was just excited about going to Wembley,' recalled Trebilcock, who has just turned 60 and who these days lives in Darwin, Lancashire, where he coaches a local club. 'I was talking with the reserve team lads about how I had dreamed about playing in a cup final, scoring a goal and how I had never thought I would get there.

'We went down to London on the Thursday and when the squad list went up I thought, "Great, I will get to sit on the bench with the other players." At Friday lunchtime the trainer said the boss wanted to see me and I thought I was going to be asked to put the kit out.

'Fred (Pickering) was in there and the manager (Harry Catterick) said: "At times like this decisions have to be made and I have to make them," and he said I was playing instead of Fred. I could have fallen off a stool – it was pretty exciting stuff.'

Trebilcock's appearance didn't just unsettle the Wednesday defence. The BBC's Kenneth Wolstenholme referred to him as 'Treble Cock' instead of 'Trebil-co' throughout his match commentary the next day when a 100,000 Wembley crowd saw one of the most dramatic fightbacks in cup final history.

Wednesday tore into their opponents from the kick-off and within twelve minutes they were ahead through their Scottish international Jim McCalliog – the first goal 'the Mersey Millionaires' had conceded in the competition that season.

The Yorkshire side doubled their lead twelve minutes into the second half when Everton goalkeeper Gordon West failed to hold a shot and David Ford snapped up the rebound. On the energy-sapping Wembley turf, Everton appeared to be a spent force but within a minute it was 2–1 when Trebilcock fired a cross from Derek Temple past goalkeeper Ron Springett for his opening goal. Suddenly the momentum was with Everton and within four minutes they had equalised when Trebilcock crashed home a shot from the edge of the box. Wednesday wilted and the winner came with sixteen minutes remaining when defender Gerry Young made a mistake and Temple raced clear to fire past Springett.

There was more drama. When a fan raced onto the pitch he was spectacularly brought to ground by a rugby tackle from a policeman who lost his helmet in the process. The crowd lapped it up, and so did the watching millions on TV, most of them oblivious to Wolstenholme's faux pas.

Only a great save by Springett denied Trebilcock when the no. 8 raced through looking for his hat-trick, but a few moments later the massed ranks of Evertonians were celebrating as Brian Labone led his team up the famous steps to collect the cup from Princess Margaret – Everton's first Wembley success since they defeated Manchester City in 1933. Soon they were indulging in a lap of honour around the track – the first time that had happened in Wembley cup final history, too.

The memories are still vivid for Trebilcock, who had also made history by becoming the first black player to score in a cup final. 'It was a fantastic day. One of my friends from home stuck his head in the team bus on the way to the stadium and held up two fingers. "You get two today Mike." And I did. We celebrated forty years ago and we're still celebrating.'

The League Cup was won by West Bromwich Albion, who defeated West Ham 5–2 in the last final to be played over two legs. Seven of the top eight

We won the cup. Everton players on the first ever Wembley lap of honour after winning the FA Cup against Sheffield Wednesday. *(PA/EMPICS)*

teams in the first division boycotted the competition (which had even less appeal forty years ago than it does now), among them the holders, Chelsea.

Northampton Town were part of English football's elite for the only time in 1965–6. The Cobblers actually won ten games and were only relegated on the final day by a goal from Bobby Robson when they lost to Fulham, who stayed up as a result. Within three seasons Northampton were back in the old fourth division.

Blackburn went down with them to be replaced by Manchester City and Southampton. The third and fourth divisions were won by Hull City and Doncaster respectively.

In fifth place in Division Three were Workington Town, a respectable achievement for one of English football's perennial strugglers at the time and especially praiseworthy that season bearing in mind that the club appointed their thirteenth director in October – which meant they had more directors than professionals on their wage bill.

In Scotland, Celtic were on the verge of greatness. Jock Stein, in his first full season in charge, was fine-tuning the team which would become the first from these shores to win the European Cup a year later. But there were domestic issues to address first. The club had not won the Scottish League title for eleven years and Celtic's fanatical support demanded that Stein and his men put that right.

In these days of the monotonous Old Firm monopoly, it is hard to believe that forty years ago provincial clubs such as Kilmarnock, Dunfermline and Hearts regularly contended and won the main Scottish honours. Those three clubs had finished 1–2–3 in the league in

> **One of football's oddest coincidences took place in a fourth division match between Chester and Aldershot when both Chester fullbacks – Ray Jones and Bryn Jones – broke their left legs. Bryn fractured his in the twenty-first minute and Ray's injury was suffered ten minutes after half-time. There were two other Joneses on the pitch that day. Chester forward Les and Aldershot's goalkeeper David. Chester, with ten men, won 3–2.**

The legendary Jock Stein was establishing Celtic as a footballing force in Scotland and beyond in 1966.
(*Keystone/Getty Images*)

1965 with Celtic a distant ninth, Stein having left Dunfermline to return to the club he had served with distinction during his playing career.

It was business as normal in 1965–6 though, and Celtic appeared to have gained the upper hand when they beat Rangers in the New Year's derby at Celtic Park, coming from a goal down at half-time to win 5–1 after fourteen tonnes of straw, which had been protecting the pitch from frost, had been removed, by Stein among others. Stevie Chalmers scored a second-half hat-trick.

John Rafferty could see the balance of power shifting towards Glasgow's east end. Writing in *The Scotsman* the following day, he declared: 'In short, Celtic, romping on the way up, passed Rangers on the way down.'

The only danger to Celtic appeared to be their punishing schedule as they fought for honours on three fronts. The return journey from a European Cup Winners' Cup tie in Tblisi took forty hours and after watching their semi-final opponents scrape a 2–2 draw against Partick Thistle to regain the lead in the title race, Liverpool manager Bill Shankly couldn't resist the opportunity of a little brinksmanship with his old pal Stein. 'I'd be more worried about facing Thistle in the semi-finals,' he chuckled.

Liverpool won 2–0 at Anfield to take the tie 2–1 on aggregate although even Shankly offered Stein a sympathetic shrug of the shoulders when Celtic had a perfectly good goal disallowed in the last minute which would have won them the tie on away goals. Stein's mood hardly improved when the Belgian referee saw TV footage of the incident and admitted he had made a mistake.

There was little opportunity to regroup. Four days later 126,552 crammed into Hampden Park to see the Old Firm Scottish Cup final finish goalless. Celtic lost the replay 1–0, but they were not to be denied the prize they craved.

Celtic knew three points from their last two games would be enough as Rangers only had one match left, which they won easily. On the same night, Alex Ferguson (yes, that Alex Ferguson), who went on to enjoy the best

> **Police in Glasgow were delighted when the first Old Firm match of the year passed off relatively peacefully with only 12 people hospitalised and 160 arrested after Celtic's 5–1 win over rivals Rangers.**

moments of his playing career at Ibrox, put Dunfermline into a surprise lead at Celtic Park. Stein's men fought back to win 2–1 and 30,000 fans staged an impromptu pitch invasion at the end. A heavy defeat in their final game would still have handed Rangers the title on goal difference, but with hundreds of supporters perched precariously on the tin roof of the stand at Motherwell's Fir Park, Celtic won 1–0 with a late goal. Rafferty summed up Bobby Lennox's clinching effort succinctly: 'It was a goal scored in the last minute of the last game on the last day of the season.'

Hamilton and Morton were relegated from Division One, with Ayr United and Airdrieonians promoted in their place.

Back at Hampden, there was no disguising the mood of hostility among the Scots as they prepared for the visit of the Auld Enemy in the Home International Championship. The Scots had failed to qualify for the World Cup finals and many laid the blame firmly at the feet of English club managers (including Shankly) for failing to release players for the make-or-break qualifier against Italy. Jock Stein took a far-from-settled side to Naples and lost, and now an expectant Scottish support wanted revenge.

John Prentice, Stein's successor as international manager – whose squad for the match had been chosen for him by a Scottish Football Association committee – was convinced that their superior individual talents would be too strong for Alf Ramsey's more prosaic English side.

Some talents did flower on that April afternoon but they were all wearing white jerseys as England silenced the 134,000 crowd with a 4–3 victory, their first over the Scots since the infamous 9–3 thrashing at Wembley five years earlier. Their margin of victory was more emphatic than the scoreline suggested.

Bobby Charlton controlled midfield and his passes enabled Geoff Hurst and Roger Hunt to put England in charge with first-half goals. Denis Law headed one back before half-time but Hunt re-established England's two-goal lead. Charlton got the fourth for an England team containing nine of the players who would enjoy Wembley glory three months later.

The manner of England's victory didn't impress everyone. Writing in *The Observer* the following day, Hugh McIllvanney was less than complimentary about the standard of the football played by both teams. 'This match produced more scoring than any international between these two countries on Scottish soil since 1880. But it had other, less welcome, distinctions.

'For a start, it is extremely doubtful if many of the meetings in those eighty-six years have thrown up so many incredible blunders. After a stirring, but totally dishevelled, hour and a half, 134,000 people were left with further proof that goals can be equated with excitement, but not quality.'

Ramsey, whose contempt for the Scots was undisguised, didn't care. His 'wingless wonders' embarked on their summer tour convinced they could win the World Cup.

CRICKET

The 1966 cricket season was all about the West Indies and the West Indies were all about Garfield Sobers. He was 30 that year, and, as batsman, three-in-one bowler, fielder and captain, at the zenith of his extraordinary powers.

If Pelé's performances in England that summer were an anti-climax, and Muhammad Ali's visits a little too fleeting, you could not say the same thing about the world's greatest cricketer.

In the Tests he scored 722 runs, including three big hundreds, at an average of 103. He also took twenty wickets and ten catches. His attacking style and athleticism took the breath away. And he led his men by vivid personal example. The West Indies, even though they were not quite the power they had been in England three years before, swept to a convincing series win on the back of his unique versatility.

The greatest cricketer ever? Many would vote for Don Bradman but Sobers, too, has a compelling case.

Sir Neville Cardus wrote in 1967: 'He is, in fact, even more famous than Bradman ever was; for he is accomplished in every department of the game, and has exhibited his genius in all climes and conditions.

'Test matches, everywhere, West Indies, India, Pakistan, Australia, New Zealand, England; in Lancashire League and Sheffield Shield cricket. We can safely agree that no player has proven versatility of skill as convincingly as Sobers has done, effortlessly, and after the manner born.'

A year after Cardus's essay Sobers embarked on a county career with Nottinghamshire that also had his rivals gasping in pursuit.

He was, without any doubt, the greatest all-round cricketer to have played the game. And in the summer of 1966 it was England's misfortune to come up against him in his prime. But even England supporters came away smiling after seeing Sobers in action. He was not fully fit when he returned to England with a weaker team in 1969 and was a little past his peak when he came, for the last time, in 1973, though he produced some memorable performances that year. But in 1966 he paraded his genius like a one-man cavalcade.

In the first Test at Old Trafford, the West Indies outplayed England and looked just as good as they had been three years before. It was all over in three days – the first time England had been beaten that quickly since Australia duffed them up at Leeds in 1938.

The West Indies won by an innings and 40 runs with the spinners dominating the match, taking 24 of the 30 wickets to fall as England's flawed selection – they only chose five specialist batsmen – was exposed.

The West Indies were fortunate to win the toss and bat first, before the pitch began to turn as terminally as a coffin screw. But their victory was so emphatic that it would be churlish to say that they were lucky.

Batting first, they scored 484, with Conrad Hunte batting for five hours to make 135 – it was Hunte, with 182, who had set up the West Indies to win the corresponding match in 1963. This time he was dropped when he had scored only seven, by Ken Higgs on the leg-side boundary. It was an expensive miss, for

Hunte's innings moulded the match which shaped the series, though Higgs had the consolation of being England's most successful bowler in the Tests.

After Hunte, Sobers destroyed the England attack to score 161, though he was dropped four times. England were bowled out for 167, with Jim Parks top-scoring with 43. Needing 317 to avoid an innings defeat, they were bowled out second time for 277. Lance Gibbs, with 5 wickets in each innings, finished with figures of 10 for 106.

In the drawn second Test at Lord's, England, for a time, had the better of things before an unbroken stand of 274, a record for the sixth wicket for the West Indies against England, between Sobers (163) and his cousin David Holford (105) turned the match on its head.

The West Indies batted first and scored 269, with Seymour Nurse making 64. When England batted the centre of interest was Tom Graveney, playing his first Test match for three years. He did not disappoint – well, he did, for he was out four runs short of his century. He put on 115 with Geoff Boycott and then Parks (91) and Basil d'Oliveira (27) took charge to lead England to 355.

Opposite: Gary Sobers (right) was the scourge of English bowlers – and batsmen – in 1966. He is pictured with Rohan Kanhai. *(Keystone/Getty Images)*

Off-spinner Lance Gibbs was a key member of the triumphant West Indies team. *(Central Press/Getty Images)*

In their second innings the West Indies collapsed to 95 for 5, a lead of just 9 runs, and their position looked hopeless. But then came that stand between Sobers and Holford, who was playing in only his second Test.

England were set 284 to win in four hours and faced the prospect of defeat when they were 67 for 4. Graveney was not going to bat because of a badly bruised right thumb but he and Colin Milburn saved the day with an unbroken stand of 130. Milburn, in ebullient form, made 126 and Holford, Gibbs and Wes Hall were all struck for six. The West Indies went 2–0 up with victory by

Fast-bowling great. The West Indies' Wes Hall. (S&G/EMPICS/Alpha)

139 runs in the Third Test at Nottingham after trailing by 90 on the first innings.

Again, Sobers led from the front, from the moment he won the toss for the third time in the series. His side looked vulnerable after being bowled out for 235 by Higgs and John Snow, with only Nurse reaching 50. England answered with 325, with Graveney striking a six and 11 fours in a memorable 109. Cowdrey almost matched him, with 96 against some hostile bowling. But their advantage did not last long.

Basil Butcher scored 209 not out, featuring in century stands with Rohan Kanhai, Nurse and Sobers, the last a violent alliance that added 173 in just two hours. The West Indies declared at 482 for 5, setting England 393 to win at 60 an hour. That's a nice dual-carriageway speed – provided you don't have Sobers, Hall, Gibbs and Charlie Griffith bowling at you.

Boycott pulled Sobers for six – yes, Boycott – and hit 6 fours in his 71, scored in two and a half hours. But after that only d'Oliveira made a half-century. England were bowled out for 253 and the defeat was particularly painful for Derek Underwood who, on his Test debut, was struck in the mouth by a bouncer from the aggressive Griffith.

The West Indies made sure of the Wisden Trophy at Headingley, where they won the fourth Test by an innings and 55 runs.

Sobers was once again at the heart of their efforts, scoring 174 and taking eight wickets for 80 runs. His captaincy was also important and he won the toss for the fourth time in as many matches – his opposite number, Colin Cowdrey, cannot have been concentrating hard enough on the coin.

The West Indies batted first and lost their first four wickets for 154. But Sobers and Seymour Nurse then dominated the England bowlers for four hours, adding 265 for the fifth wicket.

Sobers scored a century between lunch and tea in the course of his chanceless innings and also became the first Test cricketer to reach 5,000 runs and 100 wickets. It was his seventeenth Test century and his seventh against England. Nurse made 137.

The West Indies declared at 500 for nine. Then the speed of Wes Hall unsettled the England batsmen. Hall dismissed Boycott, Cowdrey and Graveney. There was resistance from d'Oliveira, whose four sixes included a straight one off Hall. But Sobers, changing from pace to spin, picked up the last three wickets in four balls and England followed on 260 behind. England made 205 second time round, losing their last five wickets for 77 as Lance Gibbs returned figures of 6 for 39.

The series was dead by the time the teams met at The Oval, but England, who had made six changes, had changed fortunes, too, and won by an innings and 34 runs.

The all-conquering West Indies team. *(Harry Thompson/Evening Standard/Getty Images)*

Tom Graveney (right) was England's batting star during a difficult summer. He is pictured with England captain Colin Cowdrey. *(Dennis Oulds/Central Press/Getty Images)*

Perhaps the most important change England made was to bring in that astute captain Brian Close, who led his country for the first time.

The West Indies batted first and scored 268, led by Kanhai (104) and Sobers (81). When England collapsed to 166 for 7 another heavy defeat looked likely. But the last three wickets added 361.

Graveney batted for six hours for his 165 and wicketkeeper John Murray looked almost as good in scoring 112 as the pair added 217. Then Snow and Higgs put on 128 for the last wicket in two hours as England took a lead of 259.

Snow dismissed both openers cheaply when the West Indies batted again but his real prize was the wicket of Sobers. Close caught him in the leg trap after instructing Snow to bowl a bouncer first ball, which Sobers attempted to hook. A great series, played in front of packed crowds, had been won 3–1 by the visitors.

The 1966 summer had provided some comfort for England supporters who embraced a new hero of their own in Colin Milburn, whose larger-than-life personality and buccaneering approach to batting finally earned him recognition beyond his county team, Northamptonshire.

Milburn, a native of the north-east, had established his reputation as an entertaining batsman after joining Northamptonshire in 1960. In his first five seasons at the County Ground he passed 1,000 runs on three occasions, but 1966 was the year when his talent truly blossomed with 1,861 runs although, curiously, fewer than 300 of them were scored on his home ground in Northampton where slow pitches inhibited his attacking zeal.

Off the field 'Ollie', as he was known, lived life to the full. He relished the social side of county cricket – meeting with team-mates and opponents for a drink after play and continuing the fun long into the evening. His 18-stone frame was proof of his love of the good things life had to offer.

By now aged 24, Milburn had done his prospects of an England call-up no harm with 64 for the MCC against a full-strength West Indies attack at Lord's in May and, the day before the first Test squad was announced, he bludgeoned 171 against Leicestershire, at the time a career-best performance.

The following day – the first Sunday when Championship cricket was played in England – Milburn received news of his selection for Old Trafford from a local press man just before taking the field to cheers from a crowd of around 5,000 for the afternoon session. In typical Ollie style, he helped sink six bottles of champagne with his team-mates afterwards before repairing to the pub for more celebrations. This was four days before a Test match, remember!

His Test career started in the worst possible manner – run out for a duck by Lance Gibbs after a misunderstanding with his opening partner Eric Russell in the second over. But after England had been forced to follow on, Milburn was determined to go down fighting. He took two boundaries off Sobers' first over and never looked back. His batting was by no means flawless and he was dropped on 52 and 87. Then, on 94 and trying to swing Gibbs out of the ground to bring up his hundred in the grand manner, he was bowled by the off-spinner. Milburn departed to a standing ovation from the 20,000 crowd. English cricket had a new star all of their own and the man himself had won the admiration of his opponents.

'We applauded him all the way,' recalled Sobers, 'for here was a man who could steal a West Indian heart.'

Ollie found himself with a new opening partner at Lord's – Geoff Boycott. The Yorkshireman recalled how, as they were padding up ready to start the innings, selector Peter May came over to him and enquired: 'You won't be trying any quick singles will you? Because I don't think Colin will make it.' Milburn made six but managed to persuade Boycott to forget about having an early night and spend the evening at Raymond's Revue Bar in London's West End instead.

In the second innings Milburn made his maiden Test hundred before England called off their pursuit of 284 to win in four hours. It was far from chanceless, but offered fantastic entertainment nonetheless. He took 12 off one over from Gibbs to go to 50 and then began hooking the tiring Hall with impunity. One blow landed 15 rows back in the Mound Stand. He chanced his arm again when Hall pitched short on 99, but instead of going square the ball flew over the slips to the third man boundary. Milburn had made his first Test hundred off just 117 balls – a phenomenal rate of progress in Test cricket in those days. A mini crowd invasion followed although efforts by four supporters to raise his considerable frame from the ground failed. He even had to decline the offer of a glass of Guinness from a spectator who had made his way over the rope from the Tavern Bar.

The next day Ian Wooldridge was fulsome in his praise in the *Daily Mail*. 'He deserves shoulder-high treatment. His innings, a blend of sweet science and basic blacksmith, contained not only the most spectacular hitting of the game but actually staved off the very real threat of defeat.'

Milburn failed in the third Test at Nottingham, as West Indies went 2–0 up, and needed hospital treatment at Headingley after he was hit on the arm during an awesome new-ball spell by Wes Hall. He returned with England 90 for 6, had a painkilling injection in his elbow and made an undefeated 29 with the tail-enders. In the second innings, as England faced certain defeat, he at least gave the crowd some entertainment with 42 quick runs.

With the series lost, the clamour for changes for the final Test at the Oval intensified. Not even a man with 316 runs in four Tests was immune, as Milburn was to discover when he was one of the players left out. 'At first I felt

Colin Milburn transferred his county form to the Test arena and gave England supporters something to smile about. *(Central Press/Getty Images)*

desperately disappointed,' he recalled. 'It seemed like the end of the world. Then I felt very, very angry. Why, I argued to myself, after scoring more runs than anyone else in the side? Why, why, why?'

His mood hardly improved when selector Alec Bedser revealed the day after the announcement that Milburn's poor fielding had cost him his place. At 18st, Milburn was no athlete and Close, the new captain and himself a fine fielder, never rated him in the field. Although the sight of him giving despairing chase to many a West Indian drive to the boundary offered the crowd some light relief in a disappointing summer, he had done most of his fielding during the series at short leg where his excellent hand-eye co-ordination enabled him to do a solid job. He hadn't dropped a catch – none had come his way, in fact – and, as his supporters in the media pointed out, he'd been chosen in the first place for his batting, not for his prowess in the field.

Discarding him seemed an illogical move, especially at a time when English cricket desperately needed new heroes who could stir the popular imagination beyond the confines of the traditional followers of the game.

It wasn't the end for Colin Milburn as a Test cricketer. He played five more times between 1967 and 1969 and finished with a very respectable Test average of 46.71. In 1969 he lost the sight of his left eye in a motor accident near Northampton and despite making a brief comeback played his last first-class game in 1974. He died in 1990 of a heart attack, aged 48.

The tour by the West Indies dominated the domestic cricket season of 1966. But before that, on the other side of the globe in the winter of 1965–6, England had already played an Ashes series against Australia, drawing the series 1–1.

The most memorable achievement of the tour was Bob Barber's wonderful 185 from only 255 balls in Sydney. But in this series even that stolid pair, Geoff Boycott and Ken Barrington, surprised everyone by playing attacking innings. Led by the popular MJK Smith, England went close to regaining the Ashes, but were ultimately let down by the form of their bowlers, though David Brown and Jeff Jones were impressive on occasions.

England got away with a draw in the opener at Brisbane, even though they were bowled out for 280 in reply to Australia's 443 for six declared (Bill Lawry 166). The second match, in Melbourne, was also drawn, even though England won a first innings lead of 200.

And so into 1966, and England started the year well. They went one up in the third match at Sydney in early January, on the back of Barber's wonderful century, and another by John Edrich. Brown (5 for 63) bowled out Australia in the first innings and the spinners, Fred Titmus and David Allen, did so in the second.

Australia, though, came back to win the fourth Test, in Adelaide, by an innings and nine runs inside four days. It was all to play for in the final match at Melbourne, then. But it was an anti-climatic draw after rain washed out the fourth day. It was hardly an anti-climax for Ken Barrington, though, who hit the fastest century of the series, from only 122 balls, nor for Bob Cowper, who built a high-rise 307 in a little over twelve hours.

Yorkshire were the outstanding county cricket team in 1966, when they won the first of a hat-trick of titles; no one from the east side of the Pennines would ever have guessed that after 1968 they would not win again until 2001.

This was their twenty-ninth title. They went top in May and appeared to be cantering home in early August when they led their closest challengers, Kent, by 40 points.

Then they won only one match in seven as Worcestershire, the champions of the previous two summers, made a charge. With only one round of matches to go, Worcestershire trailed by just 6 points, but then they were beaten by

Sussex at New Road, where John Snow and Tony Buss took eighteen wickets between them.

But this was not the greatest of Yorkshire's championship sides. Only three players, Boycott, Close and Doug Padgett, reached 1,000 runs, and they only just nudged over the line. Two bowlers, Fred Trueman and Tony Nicholson, passed 100 wickets, but Trueman was now past his spectacular pomp. Ray Illingworth topped the county's averages with eighty-five wickets at 14.51 each.

But the Championship was losing its appeal as a spectator sport after the boom years either side of the Second World War. In 1966 the administrators tampered with the laws in the hope of enlivening sterile three-day cricket by limiting the number of overs in certain games to 65, an experiment which backfired because it only encouraged bowlers and fielding sides to go on the defensive rather than look for wickets. Predictably enough, the experiment was quietly shelved after just one season.

At least one-day cricket, which was still in its infancy forty years ago, was booming and the fourth Gillette Cup final was a local derby between Warwickshire and Worcestershire, which Warwickshire won by five wickets with 3.2 overs to spare. It was, according to the *Wisden Cricketers' Almanack* of 1967, 'a tremendous struggle', though the margin looks comfortable by contemporary standards.

Three players stood out for the winners: man of the match Barber, who scored 66 out of 95, Tom Cartwright, the master medium pacer who took 3 for 16 in 12 overs, and Alan Smith, the wicketkeeper who came in late to win the game with a flurry of boundaries.

Worcestershire batted first and scored 155. Their main batsmen let them down and they slumped to 88 for 6 with Tom Graveney (18) and Basil d'Oliveira both disappointing. Norman Gifford hit two sixes and five fours in a violent 38 as 43 came from the last six overs.

Barber gave Warwickshire the start they wanted and he was well supported by Dennis Amiss (44). But the middle-order faltered until Smith seized the day, as he was to do again in the 1968 final against Sussex.

And finally, in case anyone has told you to the contrary, England won the World Cup. In 1966. No, not football, silly, but cricket.

It is forgotten now, but in September 1966 the Rothmans World Cup was played. It was not quite, perhaps, the global extravaganza that was launched in 1975, and in which England have reached three finals without ever lifting the trophy. But, until that day, 13 September at Lord's will do nicely.

This was a three-cornered tussle between England, the West Indies and a Rest of the World side, captained by Bobby Simpson.

The Rest of the World had some decent players, including the Pollock brothers, Graeme and Peter, Nadkarni, Graham McKenzie and Simpson himself. But they

Yachtsman Francis Chichester reached Sydney at the end of 1966 and was half-way to becoming the first person to circumnavigate the globe on his own. The 64-year-old mariner began his journey in his 35ft ketch Gypsy Moth in Plymouth on 27 August and headed eastwards towards Africa and the Cape of Good Hope. Chichester spent a total of 226 days at sea and completed his successful voyage on 27 May 1967 when he returned to Plymouth. He was knighted shortly afterwards and died in 1972.

Chichester had only taken up sailing at the age of 52 after a career in aviation. His boat was named after the type of aircraft he flew on a solo journey to Australia in 1929.

were betrayed by a lack of match practice and beaten by both England and the West Indies. In the final, Gary Sobers won the toss, just as he had done in the five Tests earlier in the summer, and put England in. Openers John Edrich and Peter Parfitt were in a restrained mood and at the halfway 25-overs stage England had scored just 78 for one. But a late thrash brought their score to 217 for seven.

When the West Indies batted, Colin Cowdrey, the England captain, sat in the pavilion nursing a pulled leg muscle. It was, perhaps, a blessing in disguise.

The captaincy was taken over by Ted Dexter. He was the first captain to realise that one-day cricket was most successfully played by deploying defensive fields – he had won the first two Gillette Cups for Sussex in 1963 and 1964 with these tactics, backed up by tight seam bowling.

Against the West Indies he took away the slips after the first few overs, reinstating them only at the start of a new batsman's innings. The scoring rate was strangled and England eased home by 67 runs. It was the first and last time that England won the cricket World Cup.

ATHLETICS

In August, the first Commonwealth Games which officially recognised the end of the British empire took place in hot and steamy Kingston, Jamaica. They were no longer the British Empire and Commonwealth Games although the new title of British Commonwealth Games paid due deference to the mother country.

The event forty years ago bears virtually no resemblance to the sporting extravaganza which took place in Melbourne in 2006 or indeed the Games in Manchester in 2002 when over 4,000 athletes took part from 72 countries.

In Kingston there were only thirty-four competing nations, including Saudi Arabia and Aden, and they competed in nine sports: athletics, badminton, boxing, cycling, fencing, shooting, swimming, weightlifting and wrestling. There were 1,316 athletes and officials. England topped the medal table ahead of Australia with 33 golds, 24 silver and 23 bronze. Twelve of those came from clean sweeps

High-flier. David Hemery won gold for
England in the Commonwealth Games.
(© Hulton-Deutsch Collection/CORBIS)

Mary Rand – the golden girl of British
athletics in the Sixties. *(William
Vanderson/Fox Photos/Getty Images)*

in diving and fencing, but only five were won on the track. David Hemery, an Olympic champion over hurdles two years later, won the 120 yards hurdles and Mary Rand, the reigning Olympic champion and the golden girl of British athletics in the Sixties, took the long jump. Ron Wallwork (20-mile walk), Andrew Payne (hammer) and John Fitzsimons (javelin) were England's other gold medallists. The home nations' other track golds were won by Welshman Lynn Davies in the long jump and Scot Jim Alder in the marathon.

MOTOR RACING

The Sixties was a thrilling decade for British motor-racing followers. John Surtees won in 1964, Graham Hill won twice (1962 and 1968), so did Jim Clark, perhaps the greatest of them all (1963 and 1965), and Jackie Stewart took the first of his three crowns in 1969.

So in 1966 a number of British drivers were household names, as were constructors such as BRM and Lotus-Climax. The most famous name in motor racing was still Stirling Moss, four times the runner-up in the Fifties. Now, however, there were home-grown world champions on the grid.

But 1966 was a most significant year, a time of radical change. After four years with 1.5-litre engines, a new 3-litre formula was introduced and it caught a number of manufacturers on the hop. They spent a hectic winter upgrading their machines for the new season.

The best prepared was undoubtedly the Australian Jack Brabham. He had been champion before, in 1959, with Cooper, when Britain's Tony Brooks was second, and again in 1960, with Cooper-Climax, when his nearest challenger was team-mate Bruce McLaren. In 1966, when the best five scores from only nine races counted, Brabham unveiled a new V8 engine made by Repco and it powered him to his third world title that year, ahead of Surtees. The same car was to win the title for Denny Hulme in 1967.

The 1966 season started well for the Brits at Monaco. Clark won pole position for Lotus, Surtees led for a while with Ferrari and Stewart won for BRM. The wet Belgian Grand Prix might have ended in tragedy. Eight cars retired on the first lap and one of them was Stewart, who ended upside down, trapped and drenched with petrol. This singular and intelligent man was always aware of the dangers of Formula One and even more so after this experience; the race was won by Surtees. The Brabham-Repco engine dominated for the first time in the French Grand Prix in Reims and would not release its grip for a couple of years.

Brabham went on to take the chequered flag in the British Grand Prix at Brands Hatch before winning again at Zandvoort in Holland and again at the Nürburgring, in the German Grand Prix.

Jack Brabham on his way to victory the British Grand Prix at Brands Hatch. *(Copyright © popperfoto.com)*

Formula One world champion Jack Brabham. *(Copyright © popperfoto.com)*

The Australian's luck changed when he was forced to retire at the Italian Grand Prix at Monza, but by then he had established a commanding lead over his closest rivals. He retired again in the US Grand Prix at Watkins Glen, after he had taken pole.

Clark won that race, and Surtees took the flag in the final vroom of the year in Mexico, driving for Cooper-Maserati, having fallen out with and left Ferrari. But it was Brabham's dark and handsome features which broke into a smile when all the points were added up.

Until 1966 he had not won a race since 1960. Brabham-Repco also won the Constructors' Cup, ahead of Ferrari. It was not the most powerful engine around. But it was light, reliable and compact. And it was in the hands of a master.

The legendary Mike Hailwood dominated on two wheels in the Sixties when he won nine World Championships between 1961 and 1967 and he was in his pomp in 1966 after switching to the more powerful Honda engines. He took the titles in the 250cc and 350cc class and came second in the 500cc category. Hailwood was a fearless competitor who would successfully switch to Formula One racing the following year. He achieved two podium finishes but is perhaps better known for saving the life of Clay Regazzoni whom he pulled out of a burning car during the South African Grand Prix in 1973.

Five years later and four years after retiring from Formula One, Hailwood was back on two wheels to win the Isle of Man TT title. He died in 1981 at the age of 40 in a car accident near Birmingham.

The world-famous Monte Carlo rally ended in uproar over the disqualification of the British cars who had been expected to fill the first four places. The first four finishers were Timo Makinen (Finland), driving a British Motor Corporation Mini-Cooper, followed by Roger Clark (Ford Lotus Cortina), and Rauno Aaltonen and Paddy Hopkirk, both driving BMC Minis. But they were all ruled out of the prizes – with six other British cars – for contravening regulations about the way their headlights dipped. The winner was Pauli Toivonen, a Finn who lived in Paris, driving a Citroen.

BMC and Ford lodged protests but the reputation of the rally was in tatters. One official predicted its imminent demise because the British were sure to withdraw. In the event, the rally survived and remains one of the most important races in the World Championship four decades on.

The British cars were disqualified because they used non-dipping single filament bulbs in their headlamps, in place of the standard double filament bulbs which were fitted to the version of each model which went on general sale to the public.

According to the rules introduced at the end of 1965, any car entering the rally had to come off a standard production line, with at least 5,000 cars being built to a similar specification. The British cars were equipped with standard headlamps – but the only way of dipping them was to switch to non-standard fog lamps.

The confusion arose because the rally organisers initially said the race would be run under the old rules – and only confirmed the switch after entries had been accepted.

HORSE RACING

In horse racing, a 52-year-old Australian, Scobie Breasley, resumed his successful partnership with Charlottown to win the Derby at odds of 5–1. It was the second Epsom triumph in three years for Breasley, who rode his first winner in 1928.

Fred Winter's love affair with the Grand National continued as he saddled his fourth winner in the famous steeplechase when 50/1 shot Anglo, ridden by Stan Levey, won at Aintree. Winter was the only man to win the National, Champion Hurdle and Gold Cup both as a jockey and trainer.

Scobie Breasley won his second Derby in three years at the age of 52. (Central Press/Getty Images)

Arkle, arguably the greatest steeplechaser of all time, was king of Cheltenham again after winning his third Gold Cup in March. Arkle took the lead after six fences and won by a contemptuous thirty lengths – a new record – from Dormant. Arkle's starting price was 10/1 on, the shortest in the history of national hunt's blue riband event.

RUGBY

The rugby union year was dominated by two tours: British Lions' disastrous trip to Australia, New Zealand and Canada, and the Wallabies' visit to the home nations later in 1966.

Captain Mike Campbell-Lamerton was heavily criticised during the Lions' long and disappointing tour of Australia and New Zealand. *(Keystone/Getty Images)*

The Lions' tour seemed ill-fated from the start. Welsh captain Alun Pask, whose try had helped secure an 11–6 win over England which clinched the Five Nations title in the spring, seemed to be the natural choice as skipper. Instead, the selection committee went for 32-year-old Scots Army officer Mike Campbell-Lamerton, whose own place in the team at lock forward was under threat from Ireland's Willie John McBride and who was no longer captain of his country.

The selectors compounded that mistake by selecting a manager, Des O'Brien, whose sense of priorities was such that he left the tour halfway through to go on holiday in Fiji. The coach, D.J. Robins, didn't appear to have much authority either – and even less respect from the players.

Campbell-Lamerton, who died in March 2005, wasn't helped by an itinerary which must seem laughable in today's professional era. The tour lasted just two days short of five months and featured thirty-five matches including two on the way home in Canada, one of which – against British Colombia – ended in an embarrassing 8–3 defeat.

A fractured management, a captain whose own place was under threat and tactical and selection errors were hardly a recipe for success, and so it proved – although in Australia the visitors competed well. The Lions bounced back from defeat in Sydney to draw the Test series against Australia after a 31–0 victory in Brisbane, but a New Zealand team inspired by their flinty captain Brian Lochore and the Mead brothers, Colin and Stan, who were playing together at international level for the first time, were far too strong. For the first time in Lions' history they were whitewashed 4–0 by the All Blacks. They were also beaten by four of New Zealand's provincial sides.

Robins had been appointed as the Lions' first-ever coach but there were regular disagreements with his captain over training and tactics. When the team arrived in New Zealand the local media began questioning the captain's own lack of form and Campbell-Lamerton, who was struggling with an ankle injury, eventually agreed to be left out of the team for the second and fourth Tests.

The New Zealanders wasted little opportunity in sticking the boot in – in more ways than one. Jim Telfer, one of the senior players, accused the hosts of thuggery, cheating and poor refereeing after a match against Canterbury. At the post-match dinner he said: 'I would not describe today's game as dirty because all our games in New Zealand have been dirty.'

The respected New Zealand rugby writer T.P. McLean reflected that Campbell-Lamerton had 'neither the background nor the intellectual grasp of high-level captaincy'. Switching his attention to the tour management he added: 'The Lions played shamefully badly at times, but nobody really cracked the whip. I must be blunt – the trouble was leadership.'

The captain had his supporters though. 'Mike was a decent man and much maligned,' said Brian Price, his partner in the second row for three of the internationals he played on the tour. 'We knew how hard he was working and it was because we respected his efforts that we stuck together.'

Australia arrived in the UK a few weeks later under the captaincy of John Thornett and won two of the four internationals they played. They beat England 23–11 at Twickenham and won 14–11 in Cardiff, their first-ever win over Wales and a first home defeat for three years for the Welsh. Barry John, the Llanelli fly-half, wore the famous red no. 10 jersey for the first time that day. Another debutant was Gerald Davies.

But the Wallabies lost 11–6 to Scotland and 9–6 to Ireland and the tour wasn't without its controversial moments. Hooker Ross Cullen was sent home for biting an opponent's ear.

At Wembley, St Helens beat Wigan 21–2 in front of more than 98,000 fans to win the rugby league Challenge Cup final.

TENNIS

The penultimate Wimbledon Championship before the Open era brought a new star to the attention of the sporting world. Billie Jean Moffit (who later became Billie Jean King and was to reach eight singles finals between 1966 and 1975) won the first of her six titles when she defeated Maria Bueno 6–3, 3–6, 6–1. In the men's singles Spain's Mañuel Santana defeated American Dennis Ralston in straight sets in less than two hours.

But Britain had a champion of her own, too. Ann Jones followed up her victory in the Italian Open by winning the French Open in Paris for the second time in five years. The most important hard-court title in the world belonged to Jones after she defeated the joint top seed, Nancy Richey of America, 6–3, 6–1.

GOLF

Jack Nicklaus dominated the world of golf in 1966. The Golden Bear won the fifth and sixth of his eighteen Major titles when he followed up victory at Augusta in the Masters by winning the British Open at Muirfield. It was the first Open Championship to be spread over four days. Previously, the event had to finish on Friday so that players could get back to their clubs to work in pro shops over the weekend. Nicklaus got the birdie he needed at the par-five 17th to see off the challenge of Dave Thomas and Doug Sanders. It was the first of Nicklaus's three Open triumphs and more Americans were able to enjoy their compatriot's success than ever before. Live pictures of the tournament were beamed back to the States for the first time.

Nicklaus didn't have it all his own way. Gary Player defeated him 6 and 4 in the final of the World Matchplay at Wentworth, having beaten Arnold Palmer in

Golden age. The Golden Bear Jack Nicklaus celebrates his Open triumph at Muirfield.
(Copyright © popperfoto.com)

the semi-final. The winners' purse was just £5,000 compared with the £1 million on offer in 2006.

Billy Casper won the US Open at the Olympic Club in San Francisco while the other Major, the USPGA Championship held at Firestone, Ohio, was won by the unheralded Al Geiberger whose even-par four round total of 280 was enough for a four-stroke victory. Americans filled thirteen of the top fourteen places. Player was joint third.

7

THE BOX AND BEYOND

TELEVISION

In 1966 politics was not the only greasy pole in town. Remember *It's A Knockout?* And *Batman* and *Hey, Hey It's the Monkees?* They all started that year. I see, you would rather forget them. But this was one of the great times for television.

The Sixties, under Director General Hugh Green, were the most exciting years for the cathode tube since experiments with the medium started in 1932, ten years after the British Broadcasting Company was founded. And that would remain the case until the advent of satellite and digital television and video recorders a generation later.

In 1936 a crude but regular high-definition service, the first in the world, was launched, only to be suspended three years later for defence reasons. The service was resumed in 1946 but this was still the age of radio. The coverage of the coronation of Queen Elizabeth II in 1953 changed all that. Suddenly everyone wanted television and two years later, in 1955, came the launch of ITV.

The BBC's new Television Centre at Shepherd's Bush was opened in June, 1960 and things started to move apace – broadcast had previously come from Alexander Palace and the film studios at Lime Grove.

In April 1964 there was a major breakthrough with the launch of BBC2, a channel that would take the arts seriously and cater for minority interests. It may have been promoted by the cartoon kangaroos Hullabaloo and Custard to start with, but this was serious telly.

> Over 23 million viewers tuned in to the Queen's Christmas Message, with the BBC claiming that 69 out of every 100 Britons watching the broadcast on their channel. But even Her Majesty's viewing figures were challenged later on Christmas Day when 18.8 million viewers tuned in for the highlight of the Beeb's Christmas schedules – Max Bygraves meets the Black and White Minstrels.

It was broadcast in UHF, with 625 lines. If you only had 405 lines you were a non-person. And by 1966 all the excited chatter was about colour, which would be broadcast the following year.

Colour started on 1 July 1967, though you could watch only five hours a week of it then. To get your eyes adjusted, I suppose.

A regular colour service started at the end of the year and had moved to BBC1 and ITV by 1969. Back to the year in question, we had to make do with old-fashioned monochrome, but there was some great stuff.

There was the harrowing *Cathy Come Home*, from the Wednesday Play series that had started two years before as a showcase for new playwrights and as a response to ITV's Armchair Theatre. *Cathy*, written by Jeremy Sandford and starring Ray Brooks and Carol White, dealt with the traumas of homelessness, very much in keeping with the grim, social realism of the series.

> Britain had its first pay-TV experiment in January 1966, three decades before the explosion in satellite broadcasting in this country. Opened by Anthony Wedgwood Benn, the Postmaster General, 2,500 selected viewers in London paid 19s 6d (98p) to watch two films – *Father Goose*, starring Cary Grant, and Michael Caine's *The Ipcress File* – as well as a documentary about the Royal Ballet.

It had the perfect director in the admirable Ken Loach, who learned his trade on *Z-Cars* and went on to make such films as *Poor Cow*, *Kes*, *Riff-Raff*, *Raining Stones* and, more recently, *My Name Is Joe*.

He shows life in the raw, and in *Cathy* he used hand-held cameras and documentary-style camera angles to give an enhanced realism to the story. Cathy is a northern girl who comes to London and marries Reg, a van driver. They have three children, Sean, Stephen and Marlene, but when Reg has an accident at work the family is plunged into a tortuous downward spiral.

From relatively comfortable maisonette to Reg's mum's grimy tenement, to squalid lodgings to caravan and finally to a home for the homeless, where the father is separated from his wife and children, who are then taken into care, this is the tale of a journey to helplessness and despair. There was a biting edge here. Angry viewers picked up the agenda and Shelter, the charity for the homeless, took some momentum from it.

For those who had money, *The Money Programme* started this year. It looked at the world of big business as well as what Harold Wilson described as the pound in your pocket.

There was the launch of *How!* which was presented by Fred Dinenage, Jack Hargreaves and Bunty James. It explained the workings of the world to the (mostly) young and curious and was revived in 1990 as *How 2*, presented by Carol Vorderman.

It's a Knockout – sorry to go back there, but it did have a cult following – was children's TV for grown-ups. It took place in towns all over Britain and the games were mocked up mini-wars, fought for points and infinite glory.

It was presented by Eddie Waring, of 'up and under' and 'early bath' rugby league fame, and David Vine, who eventually made way for the hysterical Stuart Hall. In these early days of the long-runner, Katie Boyle and McDonald Hobley were also involved.

There were huge beach balls, hoops, mucky puddles, outrageous climbs to clamber and jokers to play. And all the eccentric obstacles would be negotiated while wearing some madcap costume from history, or perhaps a cartoon character. If anyone tells you that TV has dumbed down in recent years point them in this direction.

Then, in 1967, came *Jeux sans frontières*, the European finals of the competition. The whole thing went on until 1982 and if that wasn't enough it was revived by Channel 5 in 1999, when Keith Chegwin and Frank Bruno starred.

Moving swiftly on, to POW! BAM! ZAP! KERRUP! In the never-ending battle to keep Gotham City safe, Adam West starred as the Caped Crusader, Batman, and Burt Ward as his sidekick Robin in what was, essentially, a moving version of the famous comic strip. The plots were absurd, the quips were awful and the over-acting occasionally painful, but the Dynamic Duo from Batcave, beneath Wayne Manor, had a popular TV following until 1968.

They would slide down their firemen's poles to their Batmobile, which was built a long time before speed cameras came on the scene. Like *It's a Knockout*, they too had a Joker, albeit a less friendly version, played by Cesar Romero, who probably preferred to be remembered for his Latin lover film roles and for his dancing. There was also The Riddler (Frank Gorshin), The Penguin (Burgess Meredith) and Catwoman (Julie Newmar). And Neil Hamilton, the old star from the latter days of the silent film era, played the always floundering Police Commissioner Gordon.

The Monkees, which also ran from 1966 to 1968, were the less-than-convincing American response to The Beatles and in particular, perhaps, the manic film *A Hard Day's Night*. More than 400 applicants were whittled down to four, three Americans and an Englishman: Michael Nesmith, Peter Tork, Mickey Dolenz and Davy Jones. They were not quite the Fab Four but for a short time they were immensely popular and there were some strong hits, including 'I'm A Believer', 'Last Train To Clarksville', 'Daydream Believer' and 'A Little Bit Me, A Little Bit You'.

Batman and Robin's adventures attracted huge TV audiences.
(Alan Band/Keystone/Getty Images)

According to the indefatigable Jeff Evans, whose *Penguin TV Companion* was quite properly described by the *Daily Mail* as 'the couch potato's bible', Jones, a young actor from Manchester, once starred in *Coronation Street* as Ena Sharples' grandson.

Then there was *Flipper*, the hero dolphin who helped see off the baddies between 1966 and 1969. Flipper's co-stars were the Florida-based brothers Sandy and Bud Ricks, who also had a pet labrador called Spray and a pet pelican called Pete but old bottle-nose was most fun.

The Frost Report started here. David Frost had made his name with *That Was The Week That Was* (1962–3), a brilliant and satirical success.

Here there was more satire, this time presented as sketches, with a particular theme each week. The best remembered sketch was one on class and featured the tall John Cleese, the average-height Ronnie Barker and the short Ronnie Corbett, who all symbolised a class level. Barker looked up at Cleese, because he was upper-class, but down on Corbett, because he was working-class.

It also starred Julie Felix, Tom Lehrer, Nicky Henson and Sheila Steafel. But the writing team was perhaps even more important. There were some famous names here and some would work together to create *Monty Python's Flying Circus* – via *At Last The 1948 Show* – a few years later.

The Python crew of Cleese, Eric Idle, Graham Chapman, Michael Palin and Terry Jones were all there, and so were Marty Feldman, Tim Brooke-Taylor and John Law. There was a compilation of *The Frost Report*, *Frost Over England*, and it won the Golden Rose at the Montreux Festival in 1967.

> The future of the satirical magazine *Private Eye* was placed in doubt in February after a court ordered them to pay £5,000 libel damages to Lord Russell of Liverpool. Editor Richard Ingram admitted: 'The atmosphere in the magazine is full of gloom.'

Another newcomer this year, and on a slightly more serious note, was *Softly, Softly*, a spin-off from the *Z-Cars* series. And it was such a successful spin-off

Opposite, top: Heads in the Sand. The Monkees – three Americans and Englishman Davy Jones – made hit records and had a successful TV show. *(Keystone/Getty Images)*

Opposite, bottom: *The Frost Report* – biting satire which attracted huge audiences. Back row, from left: Nicholas Smith, Ronnie Barker, John Cleese and Nicky Henson. Front row, from left: Julie Felix, Tom Lehrer, Ronnie Corbett and David Frost. *(Copyright © BBC)*

that it ran for ten years. Stratford Johns and Frank Windsor, as Barlow and Watt, had been upgraded to detective chief superintendent and detective chief inspector respectively. This would be called *Softly, Softly: Task Force* from 1969.

> **The State Opening of Parliament was televised for the first time in April, although MPs were unhappy at the decision. They criticised the Commons Services Committee for agreeing to the cameras without a resolution from the House.**

One of the surprise hits of the year, knocking *Coronation Street* off the top of the ratings, was *Mrs Thursday*, starring Kathleen Harrison as the eponymous heroine. For Harrison, 68, and better known as Mrs Huggett, it was a late taste of stardom. The drama was written specifically for her by Ted Willis. Her wealthy employer had died and, ignoring his grasping ex-wives, had left his considerable estate to his charlady. Hugh Manning played Richard Hunter, her aide and adviser.

Weavers Green was a sort of Archers for telly, a twice-weekly soap from Anglia. It only lasted six months but it provided an early starring role for Kate O'Mara. Grant Taylor and Megs Jenkins also starred in this story about an Australian vet running a practice in an English rural town. It was a ratings success but it was forced off air when the heavyweights from ATV wanted the slot for *Emergency Ward 10* (1957–67).

Some of the best programmes of 1966 had already been on for some time. The BBC, in particular, had a good year after struggling in the charts in previous years. But *Emergency Ward 10* was a big hit for ITV and ATV boss Lew Grade described it as one of his biggest mistakes when he took it off the air in 1967.

It was based at Oxbridge General Hospital and although the patients got a look-in occasionally – only five were allowed to die in any one year, then two – the essence of the series was the private lives of the staff. Nurse Carol Young (Jill Browne) had many admirers and so did Dr Alan Dawson (Charles Tingwell). Among the better-known patients were Ian Hendry, Joanna Lumley and Albert Finney. An old favourite, *No Hiding Place* (1959–67), was nearing the end of its long run. Before the more physical *Sweeney*, with its Flying Squad officers, came along in the Seventies this was considered the most authentic cop show in town. It starred Raymond Francis as Detective Chief Superintendent Tom Lockhart, assisted by Garry Baxter (Eric Lander) and Johnny Briggs, who was to win fame in *Coronation Street*, played D.S. Russell. It was taken off the air in 1965 but there was such an outcry that it came back for two more years.

The Power Game, formerly known as *The Plane Makers* (1963–6 and 1969), starred Patrick Wymark as John Wilder and dealt with the politics of the

The Likely Lads – James Bolam and Rodney Bewes. (*ArenaPAL Picture Library/TopFoto.co.uk*)

boardroom. *The Likely Lads* (1964–6) was one of the best of sitcoms, written by Dick Clement and Ian La Frenais, and now it is appreciated as a classic.

It starred James Bolam as Terry and Rodney Bewes as Bob, while Brigit Forsyth played Thelma, the girlfriend of the latter who would encourage him in his upwardly mobile ambitions. It centred on working-class life in the north-east, but while Terry wears his working-class origins on his sleeve and is enslaved to the pursuit of yet more beer and birds, Bob aspires to the middle class, to the world of mortgages and After Eight mints.

The pair returned for the equally successful *Whatever Happened to the Likely Lads* (1973–4). Terry has returned home after a stint in the army. Bob, who was going to join him but was disqualified on the grounds of flat feet, is now married to Thelma, and the couple are constantly embarrassed by Terry's un-reconstructed values. Like many good comedies, there is pathos among the laughs and a great deal of social realism.

Till Death Us Do Part (1966–8), by Johnny Speight, started life as a one-off in the popular Comedy Playhouse series in 1965. It had another run between 1972

Time for tea. The cast of *Till Death Us Do Part*. From left: Una Stubbs, Dandy Nichols, Tony Booth and Warren Mitchell. *(Copyright © popperfoto.com)*

and 1975 and then there was *In Sickness and in Health* (1985–92). It starred Warren Mitchell as Alf Garnett, an East End bigot who shares his house with wife Else (Dandy Nichols), daughter Rita (Una Stubbs) and son-in-law Mike, a layabout played by Anthony Booth. Mike, according to Alf, is 'a randy Scouse git', and Else nothing more than 'a silly old moo'. The selfish Garnett worships the pub, West Ham, the Queen and Winston Churchill. But he has little or no time for his family. He is a working-class Tory, which was meant to be something of a joke at the time but there must have been a few of them around judging by the election at the end of the decade.

George and the Dragon (1966–8) starred Sid James and Peggy Mount, with John le Mesurier. James plays the womanising George Russell, chauffeur and general handyman. If there are any women around he will handle them, so to speak, at least until the arrival of the formidable new housekeeper, Gabrielle Dragon (Mount).

Marriage Lines (1963–6) was an early comedy vehicle for Richard Briers, who was to become one of the most successful stars of sitcom, and Prunella Scales, who would become Sybil Fawlty in *Fawlty Towers*. They played George and Kate Starling, a young couple coming to grips with the joys and traumas (mostly the latter) of married life.

Not Only But Also starred Peter Cook and Dudley Moore. The billing is always in that order and Cook was always regarded as the creative genius behind the programme. But it was Moore to whom the BBC looked originally, inviting him to put together a one-off, jazz music-based show. Moore brought in Cook, his old friend from *Beyond the Fringe*, and the show became a series, best known for its Pete and Dud dialogues.

From America there came *The Dick Van Dyke Show* (1963–7). Van Dyke plays Rob Petrie, a writer for the Alan Brady Show, with his wife, Laura, played by Mary Tyler Moore. This was an early example of the popular, wisecracking sitcoms that would flow from the US.

The Munsters (1965–7) had Fred Gwynne as Herman Munster, who looks remarkably like the monster created by Dr Frankenstein. He is the head of a friendly but ghastly looking family – they're a lot worse than *The Addams Family*, who were about at the same time. For fans of the Western there was *The Virginian* (1964–73) which ran at feature length and starred James Drury as the eponymous hero, with Doug McClure as his younger friend, Trampas.

This was a thoughtful, moralising series that ran a little deeper than the normal fist fights and shoot-outs that take up so much time in the genre. There were a number of celebrity guest appearances from the likes of Bette Davis, Charles Bronson and George C. Scott. *Dr Finlay's Casebook* (1962–71) was at the height of its popularity at this time. It starred Bill Simpson and Andrew Cruickshank as the Tannochbrae doctors and Barbara Mullen as their housekeeper, Janet. The stories reflected the conflict between the eager young professional (Finlay) and his grumpy elder colleague, Dr Cameron. The endearing tales, by A.J. Cronin, were originally published as *The Adventures of a Black Bag* and were recently adapted for Radio 4.

Dr Kildare (1961–6) was getting ready to snap his black bag shut for good. Kildare (Richard Chamberlain) worked at the Blair General Hospital and his Dr Cameron was Dr Gillespie, played by Raymond Massey. Again, the theme was a dedicated and idealistic young doctor coming up against moral and ethical dilemmas.

Another doctor going strong around this time was *Doctor Who*, which started in 1963 and is popular again today. This was the year that the original time traveller, William Hartnell, mutated into craggy-faced Patrick Troughton, a Shakespearean actor and, for many, the best Who of the lot. Dr Who is more famous for having a silly scarf round his head than a stethoscope, and he is more likely to give you sleepless nights than help cure them. But from the time it first reached the screen, on the day after President Kennedy was assassinated in November 1963, until the present day, it has been one of the iconic TV programmes for children and adults alike. At tea-time on Saturday there was nothing else to do but marvel at the good doctor as he wrestled with the Daleks, the Cybermen and low-budget special effects.

There were more conventional heroes around at this time. *The Saint* (1962–9) starred the pre-Bond Roger Moore as the smoothie Simon Templar, who seemed to travel the world in his white Volvo P1800 and always seemed unfazed when a halo suddenly appeared above his head. *The Man From U.N.C.L.E.* (1964–8) made the most of the James Bond craze when Sean Connery was 007. It starred Robert Vaughn and David McCallum as Napoleon Solo and Illya Kuryakin and there were gadgets galore.

Patrick Troughton – one of the better doctors. *(TopFoto.co.uk)*

The American Solo (whose name can be found in the Bond film, *Goldfinger*) and the Russian Kuryakin, who answered to an elderly English boss, Mr Waverly, played by Leo G. Carrol, are agents fighting crime, usually represented by the international syndicate called THRUSH.

The Informer starred Ian Hendry as Alex Lambert, who passed on all he knew to D.S. Piper, played by Neill Hallett. Hendry is a disbarred barrister who plays life on the edge. *The Corridor People* (1966) lasted for only four episodes but had a following. It was a thriller series with a difference in which John Sharp played Kronk, a CID man who is after Syrie Van Epp, a mysterious Persian woman.

Steve Forrest starred as *The Baron*, aka John Mannering (1966–7), a jet-setting American arts dealer who drives a Jensen and also works as an undercover agent, especially when the crime involves the theft of something precious. Then there was Patrick McGoohan as *Danger Man* John Drake (1960–8). Drake works for NATO early on. But then he becomes a member of the British Secret Service and, as if James Bond has infiltrated his persona, we see much more gadgetry.

Get Smart (1965–7) was a cross between Bond and the bumbling Inspector Clouseau. He is an American, Maxwell Smart, played by Don Adams, a secret agent whose headquarters, ten storeys below street level in Washington DC, are accessed through the bottom of a telephone kiosk.

More popular than all of these were *The Avengers* (1961–9) which had a strong cult following. It starred Patrick MacNee as John Steed. And by now Cathy Gale (Honor Blackman) had made way, in 1965, for Steed's most famous partner, Emma Peel (Diana Rigg). While Steed doffs his bowler and twirls his rolled umbrella the leather-clad Peel races around in a Lotus Elan, dispensing karate chops in all directions. The zany, imaginative plots usually concern evil megalomaniacs who for some reason appear to concentrate their attention in small, British rural communities.

The Avengers made PC George Dixon (*Dixon of Dock Green*, 1955–76) appear a little staid. But Jack Warner, reprising his film role in *The Blue Lamp*, was one of the most enduring of all TV stars and Dixon ran for twenty-one years. He was the sort of old school copper we would all like to see at the bottom of the road, not shooting or fitting up anyone but working as a sort of uniformed social worker, assisting everybody and everything but always ready to provide a clip round the ear if things got out of hand.

From America, though, came someone with even more clout than Dixon, Steed or Danger Man. Samantha Stevens (Elizabeth Montgomery) starred in *Bewitched* (1964–76), about a contemporary witch who could solve any problem with a twitch of her nose, although her long-suffering husband, Darrin (Dick York at this time) is dubious about the whole thing and wears a permanently anxious expression.

This hit series was based on the film *I Married a Witch* (1942), which was based on the Thorne Smith novel of the previous year, *The Passionate Witch*. York, though, suffered from back problems all his life and there was much confusion when he was replaced by Dick Sargent in later episodes.

There was no problem about finding substitute actors in *The Flintstones* (1961–6), a popular cartoon series that was usually watched on late Saturday afternoon. It starred Fred and Wilma, supported by the Rubbles, Barny and Betty, and they lived in Bedrock a million – or more – years BC. The scripts were clever and a running gag was the way in which these ancients had all the modern gadgets, albeit with a less sophisticated design (the beak of a prehistoric bird doubled as a record stylus, and cars relied on their owners' feet, not wheels, to move along).

Double Your Money, starring Hughie Green and Monica Rose, was one of ITV's most popular game shows. *(Copyright © popperfoto.com)*

The daddy of all the children's shows was *Blue Peter*, a magazine programme that started in 1958 and was at the peak of its popularity at this time. At the end of December, 1965, John Noakes joined the regular presenters Christopher Trace and Valerie Singleton and his daring escapades gave the show a new lease of life.

Jackanory (1965–96) was aimed at younger children and its simple format was to have someone reading a book. More than 700 books were read, one a week in five, 15-minute slots, and the well-known readers included Kenneth Williams and Bernard Cribbins.

Ready Steady Go! (1963–6) was coming to an end on ITV, a pop music showcase presented by Keith Fordyce, David Gell, Michael Aldred and Cathy McGowan. Music hall was dead by the mid-Sixties. And little wonder. It had moved to television. There were a number of variety shows among the year's most popular programmes. The most successful of these had always been *Sunday Night at the London Palladium*, a spectacular that had already made Bruce Forsyth and his chin famous. But even more popular this year was *A Royal Gala*, a 150-minute show-case for ITV. Here, the traditional variety entertainers were joined by stars from *Coronation Street*, *Emergency Ward 10*, *Double Your Money* and *Ready Steady Go!*

There was also *Secombe and Friends*, in which Harry Secombe did more than just invite on his fellow goons Peter Sellers and Spike Milligan. The host always seemed to have a number of Welsh friends along, such as Richard Burton, Stanley Baker, Donald Houston and singer Geraint Evans, who ended up singing in the shower with Harry. *The Morecambe and Wise Show* always had a strong variety element. There was always plenty of music, provided by the likes of Jackie Trent, The Settlers, The King Brothers and The Shadows.

The Hippodrome mixed circus acts with quality music, provided by the likes of The Everly Brothers and Dusty Springfield. *The Blackpool Show*, hosted by Tony Hancock, brought a whiff of the seaside into the living room from the ABC Theatre. Game shows had been long established by this time. New Zealander Michael Miles had been exhorting everyone to *Take Your Pick* since the start of ITV eleven years earlier, pleading with contestants to take the money or open the box. The show had been brought over from Radio Luxembourg and you would get gonged out if you said 'yes' or 'no'. *Double Your*

> The BBC confirmed that it would start broadcasting television programmes in colour from 1967, making Britain the first country in Europe to offer regular programmes in colour. Postmaster General Anthony Wedgwood Benn made the announcement in the Commons and said that providing four hours of colour programming a week, initially on BBC2, would cost £1–2 million a year. The amount of colour broadcasts would increase to ten hours a week by 1968.

Money, another import from Luxembourg, had the same lifespan as *Take Your Pick* (1955 to 1968) and was presented by Hughie Green. It was based on the American programme, *The $64,000 Dollar Question*, and Green had a number of assistants, including the popular Monica Rose.

In 1966 the twelve most popular TV programmes were:

1. *Miss World*, BBC1, an audience grabber for years until political correctness frowned upon it. In 1966 it was watched in 9.80 million homes.
2. *Mrs Thursday*, ITV, 9.55 million
3. *Royal Gala*, ITV, 9.55 million
4. *Secombe and Friends*, ITV, 9.45 million
5. *London Palladium Show*, ITV, 9.15 million
6. *Coronation Street*, ITV, 9.05 million
7. *Double Your Money*, ITV, 8.85 million
8. *Take Your Pick*, ITV, 8.80 million
9. *The Rat Catchers*, ITV, 8.50 million
10. *No Hiding Place*, ITV, 8.45 million
11. *The Avengers*, ITV, 8.40 million
12. *Cinema*, ITV, 8.30 million

But a feature of the period was not merely the popularity of programmes. This was a golden era for programme makers who were not necessarily dictated to by the viewing figures.

David Attenborough was appointed Controller of BBC2 in 1965 and a number of initiatives flowed from his creative imagination. *The World About Us* and *Civilisation* were yet to come but the arts magazine programme *Line-Up*, and then *Late Night Line-Up* (1964–72), presented by the likes of Joan Bakewell, Denis Tuohy, Sheridan Morley and Tony Bilbow, were early examples of how good and ruminative BBC2 could be. On balance, though, we preferred *The Avengers*.

RADIO

By now, TV had asserted itself ahead of radio as the main means of home entertainment. For this reason, we have devoted less space to what represented the original meaning of wireless. But radio was still a vitally important medium in terms of news and entertainment. And, unlike television, it continued to employ the user's imagination – there was even a radio programme called *A Tribute to the Silent Screen*.

This was the last full year of the Light Programme, which started life in 1945 and ran until 30 September 1967, when it was replaced by a combination of Radio 1, on its medium-wave frequencies, and by Radio 2, the new name for the programme, on long wave. The Light Programme concentrated on light entertainment and music and its favourite programmes included *Beyond Our Ken* (which would become *Round The Horne*) *The Clitheroe Kid*, *Educating Archie*, *The Al Read Show*, *Children's Favourites*, *Dick Barton*, *Does the Team Think?* and *Friday Night is Music Night*.

Then there was *Housewives' Choice*, *Have A Go*, *Meet the Huggetts*, *Merry-Go-Round*, *Much Binding in the Marsh*, *The Navy Lark*, *Music While You Work*, PC 49, *The Billy Cotton Bandshow*, *Life With the Lyons*, *The Man in Black*, *Hancock's Half Hour*, *ITMA*, *Listen With Mother*, *Woman's Hour*, *Worker's Playtime*. . . .

Pirate radio stations had a reprieve for another year after the government decided not to introduce legislation to outlaw them until adequate local broadcasting services were in place.

This was also the era of the pirate radio stations, long before Radio 1 got going. If you're looking to blame someone for the arrival of Tony Blackburn this is the way to go. And radios were even beginning to look different. The large piece of furniture, with warm-up valves, had made way for the transistor radio revolution.

Transistors had appeared in America from 1954 and in Britain from 1956. The first transistor radio to be imported from Japan was the Sony TR620, which measured $1\frac{1}{4} \times 3\frac{1}{2}$in. And there were soon plenty more that would fit in your top pocket, including the Stellar, Gaiety, Champion, Harmony and Hi-Sonic.

The Archers, the biggest radio star of them all, was first heard nationally on the Light Programme in January 1951, though it had already been broadcast in the Midland regional service of the Home Service in 1950.

Another popular radio drama series on the Light Programme in those days was *Mrs Dale's Diary*, which followed *Morning Story*, which followed *Music While You Work*. A number of Light Programme announcers are still fondly remembered, including Franklin Engelmann, Jean Metcalfe, Marjorie Anderson, Roy Williams and Robert Dougall. The Home Service, which would become Radio 4, ran from 1939 until September 1967.

Unlike Radio 4 it had regional variations and was broadcast on medium wave. Some of its best known announcers were Ronald Fletcher, Wallace Greenslade, Frank Phillips, Joy Worth, Kenneth Kendall and Harry Middleton and some of its favourite programmes were *In Town Tonight* and *The Brains Trust*.

So what would you have done on Saturday 30 July 1966 if you had wanted to avoid the World Cup? If you had chosen to spend the day with the Light

Programme you had to start early, at 5.30 a.m., with *Breakfast Special*, three hours of big band music.

This was followed at 8.33 – yes, 8.33! – by *Children's Favourites*, a popular request programme for the kids presented, at this time, by John Ellison. *The News at Five to Ten* was followed, at ten, by *The Saturday Club*, presented by Brian Matthew, that enduring star of Saturday morning radio. This was a great success. It was another request programme, mixed with some new releases.

David Frost at *The Phonograph*, at noon, was followed by *Music Parade* at 1.30, in which the Radio Orchestra would play a selection of popular melodies. And it was music all the way in those days. *Swing Into Summer* came on at 2.15, followed by *Saturday Bandstand* at 3.45. Then, at 4.30, there was *Music From The Movies*. At five o'clock Jimmy Shand presented a miscellany of music from Scotland, called *Heather Mixture*.

There was some light relief at 5.31 when Joan Turner presented her own very personal brand of humour. At 6, Northern Variety Parade presented *The Billy Dainty Show*. There was more music with *Sweet and Savage* at 6.30, followed by the news and *Radio Newsreel* at 7 and sport, with the close of play cricket scores, at 7.25. There was some more music at 7.30 when Geoffrey Wheeler presented *Blackpool Night*.

More comedy followed with *I Was Walking up the Road*, with Jimmy Hanley, at 8.30, followed by the *Henry Wood Promenade Concert* at 8.50. The Radio Dance Orchestra played at 10 and this was followed by Simon Dee, Lennie Felix and the news at 2 a.m., followed by close-down at 2.02. Easy-going music was the dominant force. So you would have been much better off watching the World Cup after all.

A glance at some of the most popular radio programmes running on the Home and Regional Home Services in July 1966 shows us that *The Archers* was not the only one that survived. There was *Farming Today*, *Today's Papers*, *Yesterday in Parliament*, *The Daily Service*, *Pick of the Week*, *The World at One* and *Book at Bedtime*, among others – which is pretty comforting when you think about it.

And radio is comforting, among many other things. You only realise how outstanding Radio 4 is when you are ill in bed, and the same applied to the Home Service in those days. Even more so, because it was more 'old school' at that time and the broadcasters sounded like doctors with a friendly bedside manner.

While television took hold in the evenings the mornings – and at the weekend they were long mornings – belonged to radio. And then there was Sunday lunchtime comedy. The Sunday roast just wasn't the same without the *Navy Lark*, Kenneth Horne, Jimmy Clitheroe and Al Read. It didn't matter that the lamb was overdone because everyone was laughing so heartily.

Quite the funniest programme on radio at this time, in our subjective opinion, was *Round the Horne* (1965–9), the successor to *Beyond Our Ken*. Kenneth Horne, whose premature death in February 1969 brought the series to a close, was the honey-voiced ringmaster for a number of madcap circus acts.

The best known and most versatile of these was Kenneth Williams who played, among other parts, Rambling Syd Rumpo and Peasemold Gruntfuttock. He was also half of Julian and Sandy, with Hugh Paddick. Betty Marsden also starred as, among others, Dame Celia Molestrangler. Barry Took and Marty Feldman were among the writers and the programme enjoyed the hallmark of distinction: Mary Whitehouse, the broadcasting standards campaigner, had serious misgivings.

It was simply outrageous, a combination of innuendo and camp comedy that was quite daring for the time. And there were just simple but gorgeous pieces of word-play.

'Do you charge your patients, doctor?' 'Certainly not! I just sidle up to them.' Wonderful.

The *Navy Lark* was radio's longest-running sitcom. There were fifteen series between 1959 and 1976 – and then the crew of *HMS Troutbridge* made a reappearance in a Jubilee special in 1977. It was originally written as a vehicle for John Pertwee. A young Ronnie Barker also made a name for himself here. And then there was Leslie Phillips as the maladroit Sub-Lieutenant. 'Left hand down a bit!' became a familiar catchphrase. It was always followed by a desperate shout from Pertwee to take avoiding action. And then there came the smash. 'I caused more damage to naval property than the Navy had done in two world wars,' Phillips said. The series was written by Laurie Wyman, who also wrote, on occasions, for Tony Hancock.

Hancock's Half Hour was really a hit of the Fifties. In 1966 the tragic Tony Hancock had just two years to live, but *Hancock's Half Hour* was so good it was repeated throughout the Sixties. Written by Ray Galton and Alan Simpson, who were to script the *Steptoe and Son* series, it positioned Anthony Aloysius St John Hancock at 23 Railway Cuttings, East Cheam. His frustrated life was summed up by the catchphrase: 'Stone me, what a life.' If he didn't frustrate himself, with his pomposity and rather immature ambitions, there was always Sid James at hand to push him in the general direction of disaster. Hattie Jacques and Kenneth Williams were also around to lend an unhelpful hand. Such episodes as 'The Blood Donor', 'Twelve Angry Men', 'Radio Ham', 'The Set That Failed' and 'The Reunion Party' remain classics.

If *The Clitheroe Kid* was less obviously funny, it also had a very long run (1958–72), and there were seventeen series. The 4ft 3in Jimmy Clitheroe, from the town of the same name, played a schoolboy who was always getting into trouble. It was written by James Casey and Frank Roscoe. Tony Melody played

Mr Higginbottom, Diana Day and Judith Chalmers his long-suffering elder sister, Susan, and Renée Houston and Patricia Burke his mother.

Al Read, another favourite accompaniment to the Sunday roast, was a Salford sausage-maker who is best remembered for such phrases as 'Right monkey' and 'You'll be lucky'. He was very popular throughout the Fifties and Sixties.

Very different was *Does the Team Think?* This was a light-hearted version of the serious discussion programmes that were beginning to proliferate on radio and TV at the time. And, a little like the *News Quiz* today, it relied on the wit and humour of the panel, for this was a largely unscripted show. The three regulars on the panel were Jimmy Edwards, Ted Ray and Arthur Askey. The guest slot would be filled by the likes of Cyril Fletcher, Tommy Trinder, Irene Handl or Bernard Bresslaw. And then we come to *Children's Favourites*. I know this is beginning to sound a little like Orson Welles in pursuit of Rosebud, but *Children's Favourites* was a great programme. It ran from 1954 until the Light Programme went belly-up in 1967. Derek McCulloch was the original Uncle Mac, and on Saturday mornings he would play all the songs kids wanted to hear.

'Hullo children, everywhere,' he would say at the start. And sometimes you might even hear your name read out. The favourite songs included 'The Laughing Policeman', 'Little Red Monkey', 'Buttons and Bows', 'The Runaway Train', 'When You Come to the End of a Lollipop', 'Nellie the Elephant', 'How Much is that Doggy in the Window?', 'The Ugly Duckling', 'I Know an Old Lady', 'The Three Little Fishes', 'A Four-Legged Friend', 'Sparky's Magic Piano', 'Little White Bull' and many, many others.

Saturday mornings would always be just like this, or so we thought. But then, as the programme and some members of its audience started to age, there was Gerry and the Pacemakers and The Beatles and it wasn't the same any more. Uncle Mac had gone, too, replaced by the more informal Ed Stewart, who mixed current single hits with the old favourites.

FILMS

After the romantic blockbusters of the previous year, *The Sound of Music* and *Doctor Zhivago*, the cinema became a little more poker-faced in 1966. There was one runaway winner, at least according to the Oscars. Fred Zinnemann's *A Man for All Seasons*, based on Robert Bolt's 1960 play, starring Paul Scofield as Sir Thomas More, almost swept the board. As the *Radio Times Guide to Films* had it, 'More wins the moral argument but loses the more vital one, concerning custody of his head.'

There were a number of fine performances here, including a cameo from Orson Welles as Cardinal Wolsey that almost stole the show. Leo McKern is excellent as Thomas Cromwell, as is Robert Shaw as Henry VIII – and, in parliament, John Hurt also catches the eye in his first major role. But this is Scofield's picture. One of the greatest stage actors of his time, he never did become a glitzy film star. As David Thomson pointed out in his seminal *The New Biographical Dictionary of Film*, 'Scofield has a face that was never quite young or sociable.' He was a memorable King Lear (Peter Brook, 1970) and more recent filmgoers will recall his performances in *Quiz Show* (Robert Redford, 1994) and *The Crucible* (Nicholas Hytner, 1996). But it was playing More that won him his Oscar, a towering performance that married moral conviction with vanity; no wonder he lost his head.

A Man for All Seasons also won best picture at the Academy Awards. And Zinnemann picked up another of those little gleaming statues for his directing. Zinnemann, famously, had directed *High Noon* (1952), *From Here to Eternity* (1953) and *Oklahoma!* (1955). But *A Man for All Seasons* was perhaps best suited to his qualities of seriousness, even solemnity. *The Day of the Jackal* (1973) was the best known of his subsequent films.

While Zinnemann and Scofield were conquering Hollywood, *Who's Afraid of Virginia Woolf?* won Best Film in Britain, though it also won Oscars for, among others, Elizabeth Taylor (Best Actress) and Sandy Dennis (Best Supporting Actress). Directed by Mike Nichols from Edward Albee's coruscating and biting stage play about domestic disharmony, it starred Taylor and Richard Burton as the feuding married couple – they were also man and wife in real life by then.

> There were two surprises at the Oscars in Hollywood. Best Actor went to Lee Marvin for his portrayal of a drunk in the Western spoof *Cat Ballou* while Julie Christie took Best Actress for her portrayal of a London model in *Darling*, which was filmed in black and white. The film also picked up the award for Best Screenplay and Best Costume Design. Christie received almost as much publicity for what she was wearing when she accepted the award from Rex Harrison – a gold lamé trouser suit. It was the first time a woman had accepted an Oscar award while not wearing an evening gown. The Best Film Oscar went to *The Sound Of Music*.

Those who have seen Burton on stage say he was a great actor, an argument his rather hammy film roles have difficulty in sustaining. Great voice, great eyes, but what else? This film, though, provides strong performances from both its main stars. If you have ever felt nervous about holding a dinner party this film puts you off the notion of even attending one. The guests are caught in a fusillade of verbal volleys from Burton and Taylor and they look as if they would rather be hit by flying crockery. It was something of a practice run for the two leading players, who would split a few years later, making as much noise as a Formula One grand prix.

Mike Nichols would go on to make *The Graduate* (1967), *Working Girl* (1988) and *Regarding Henry* (1991). But this was the film that made his name as a director. Nichols and Zinnemann were responsible for the films that cleaned up at the awards ceremonies but there were many others that became talking points in 1966.

Another nasty piece of realism, insofar as it reflected the bleak side of the new promiscuity, was *Alfie*, starring that former Smithfield meat-market porter Michael Caine. If you have seen the recent remake it's not a patch on the original. Caine may not be everyone's favourite film star, and he was to have more success as a supporting actor, but in films such as *Alfie* and *Get Carter* (1971) he proved he could lead the cast most effectively.

In *Alfie*, he plays a self-centred lady-killer, a cold-eyed, Cockney seducer combining charm, callousness and naïvety. He seems indifferent to the suffering he has caused. The abortion scene is particularly painful to watch. There are several strong supporting performances in Lewis Gilbert's film, notably from Julia Foster, Millicent Martin and Vivien Merchant.

On a lighter note, there was *The Fortune Cookie*, in which Billy Wilder teamed Jack Lemmon and Walter Matthau for the first time. The film is also known as *Meet Whiplash Willie*. TV cameraman Harry (Lemmon) gets knocked out at a football game. Matthau, who won an Oscar for his portrayal of Willie, the shyster lawyer and Harry's brother-in-law, sees the chance of making some easy money. He persuades Harry to feign paralysis and claim damages. The humour and cynicism between the two, which were to be replicated in *The Odd Couple* (1968) and *The Front Page* (1974), were as sharp here as in any of their many collaborations. Matthau is at his lugubrious best – and gets most of the good lines. Lemmon is gullible and innocent, but not without blame himself. We see him here in the sort of morality-questioning role that would define much of his career, a great comedy actor who was capable of getting serious.

The great Vienna-born Wilder, one-time tabloid journalist and, in his own words, 'a gigolo', the man who arrived in Hollywood with little money and less English, the maker of such grim parables as *Double Indemnity* (1944), *The Lost Weekend* (1945) and *Sunset Boulevard* (1950), but also such hilarious films as *Some Like It Hot* (1959), had made yet another memorable contribution to his industry. And in Lemmon and Matthau, who became good friends, he brought together two gifted actors who would go on making films together for more than thirty years.

The *Carry On* films represented another reliable source of mirth in the 1960s, when they were at the height of their popularity. Often considered as vulgar, low-brow comedy, they were nonetheless regularly watched. The bawdiness of plot sometimes disguised the fact that the writing was very clever and, delivered by Kenneth Williams, Kenneth Connor, Sidney James, Joan Sims, Hattie Jacques, Charles Hawtrey, et al, often sidesplittingly funny.

For many, *Carry On up the Khyber* (1968) was a favourite but, in 1966, *Carry On Screaming* and *Carry On: Don't Lose Your Head*, both scripted by Talbot Rothwell, were considered two of the better examples of the genre. The first starred Williams as Dr Watt, the mad scientist of clichéd legend, in a spoof of the Hammer horror films. In his only *Carry On* film, there was also a memorable performance by Harry H. Corbett, as the detective, and by Fenella Fielding, as a vampire.

Carry On: Don't Lose Your Head, a spoof of *The Scarlet Pimpernel*, was not originally intended as one of the series, though it was made by the *Carry On* director Gerald Thomas. And it sees James and Williams at their ribald best. There are not many laughs in the *The Good, the Bad and the Ugly*. Not intentionally, anyway. This was the third and last of Sergio Leone's 'dollar' or 'spaghetti' Westerns. It stars Clint Eastwood, Eli Wallach and Lee Van Cleef, and there is the same stylised bloodshed and mayhem as before. The setting is the American Civil War and the buried treasure plot is hardly original. But there is some decent black humour, too, as well as some wry, dry comments about human nature.

Eastwood, poncho and cheroot in place, is at his impassive best as the Man With No Name who was becoming a very big name indeed in the cinema. These were the films that made Eastwood – and Leone – a star, before he became a little more talkative in his 'Go ahead, make my day' *Dirty Harry* series.

Georgy Girl, like *Alfie*, was very much a film of its time and was considered daring. It starred Lynn Redgrave as a lonely dance teacher who is offered an amorous escape from tedium by James Mason, her married employer, but who finds greater fulfilment looking after the illegitimate baby of her flatmate, played by Charlotte Rampling.

Alan Arkin starred in *The Russians are Coming*, which was good enough to win an Oscar nomination as best picture. In a Cold War setting, Arkin plays a Russian who grounds his submarine off the American coast and strolls ashore looking for assistance, unaware of the panic he is about to unleash.

Morgan, a Suitable Case for Treatment, is another film about one of the angry young men whose strident cries were often heard in the theatres and cinemas of the 1950s and 1960s. This one, adapted from the television play by David Mercer, deals with class war. Artist David Warner decides to sabotage the second marriage of his wife, played by Vanessa Redgrave, by dressing up in a gorilla suit and re-wiring their house. There are some funny moments which add up to something less than a satisfying whole and which now look a tad dated.

Harold Pinter wrote the screenplay of the stylish *The Quiller Memorandum*, a Len Deighton spy thriller starring George Segal, Alec Guinness and Max von Sydow. It was an impressive piece of work with some fine acting.

The Sand Pebbles won eight Oscar nominations, but did not carry off one of them. It stars Steve McQueen in one of his less remembered roles and goes on for over three hours. It is set in China in 1926, aboard a US gunboat patrolling the Yangtze River. The most memorable aspect of the film is the terrific camerawork by Joseph MacDonald. Talking of wonderfully shot films, *Born Free* is right up there, the moving story of Joy and George Adamson, played by Virginia McKenna and Bill Travers, and their battles to raise the lion cub Elsa and then deal with the animal's growing maturity. It was a tear-jerker that picked up two Oscars and its theme song, memorably performed by Matt Munro, is an enduring favourite.

There is a nice line in *The Professionals*. Ralph Bellamy says: 'You bastard!' And Lee Marvin replies: 'In my case as accident of birth, but you, Sir, are a self-made man.' It's a violent Western from Richard Brooks with shades of Sam Peckinpah's *The Wild Bunch*, who were to gallop along three years later.

Michael Keaton made Batman famous on screen but the Caped Crusader made his cinematic debut as a spin-off from the popular TV series, which also starred Adam West and Burt Ward. It stands up well to its glitzier successors and there are plenty of familiar gags.

The special effects forty years ago were a little primitive by today's standards, so *Fantastic Voyage* was exactly that for director Richard Fleischer. He shrunk a team of doctors, placed them in a mini-sub and injected them into the bloodstream of a dying Czech scientist. The craft is thrown about by the tidal waves and winds of the inside of the body. It could have been worse, but luckily for the crew the Czech boffin didn't seem to bother with takeaway curries. Shrinking Raquel Welch might not be everyone's idea of a clever notion but this was a fun film, even though the laboured script didn't quite match up.

Director Sergei Bondarchuk had slightly loftier intentions when he was given the job of making Tolstoy's *War and Peace* (1967). If you are short of time, read the book – it will be quicker. The Soviet film industry and the Red Army were made available to Bondarchuk – and so were 20,000 extras. The result was a film lasting 507 minutes in its original Russian version, though this was cut to a sleeker 399 minutes. There were some great battle and ballroom scenes though. But how did Bondarchuk find time to play one of the leading parts, that of Pierre Bezuhov?

A lot less serious is *King of Hearts*, which attracted a cult following. It is set in the Great War and stars Alan Bates, who stumbles across a town of madmen which is due to be carpet-bombed at midnight. Well, OK, you may have to place tongue in cheek, but there are some nice satirical swipes here, in all directions, and the French cast is superb.

The *Round-Up*, from Hungary, centres on the 1848 revolt against Hapsburg rule. It is about the bravery of resistance and the sadism of the police in a totalitarian state. There are no real villains, or heroes; you can place the white or black hat on the head of whoever you choose.

Hunger, a Norwegian/Swedish language film, is an adaptation of that wonderful writer Knut Hamsun's first novel of the same name. It is about art, or more specifically about the stubborn creative pride of a writer, who suffers near-starvation and much anxiety because of his craft.

Death of a Bureaucrat, a lovely black comedy from Cuba, has some sharply satirical bites at Castro and it is a minor surprise that it ever got released. Perhaps Fidel, who has seen off various American attempts to unseat him over fifty years, felt confident and magnanimous.

Back in English, *The Chamber of Horrors* was made as a pilot for a TV series but was then considered too nasty to show. The horror genre often evokes more titters than screams but this effort has some seriously gruesome moments, not least when Patrick O'Neal, the Baltimore Strangler, cuts off his own manacled hand to escape the police. Some extra nasty bits were put in for cinema audiences and there were Horror Horns and Fear Flashers to tell you when to shut your eyes.

James Mason was one of the most interesting British talents of his time and by now he had moved on from his wartime roles, in which he played handsome and intelligent villains with a hint of real menace. In *The Deadly Affair* he plays an intelligence officer with a difficult private life who investigates a colleague's suicide in an adaptation of the John Le Carré novel, *Call for the Dead*. Director Sidney Lumet, who did a lot of work with Mason, was on fine form, too.

The busy New Yorker Lumet, who seemed capable of wringing great performances from his actors, also directed *The Group*, based on the novel by Mary McCarthy, charting the personal development of eight women leading up to the Second World War. *The Chase*, from Bonnie and Clyde director Arthur Penn, has a young Robert Redford as an escapee from choky who is protected by a Texan sheriff, played by Marlon Brando. It sounds a cliché of a plot but this is a powerful tale of a town's hatred and guilt.

The Wild Angels, the first of the biker movies, stars Peter Fonda, and you find yourself wishing his dad, Henry, would come along and give him a clip round the ear. It's a Hell's Angels film and an orgy of violence, drug-taking and gang-rape, while the documentary style of its shooting makes it more shocking still. It's enough to make you give up your leathers, buy a scooter and become a mod.

A little more gentle, and certainly a film of its time, is *The Family Way*, starring Hayley and John Mills, Hywel Bennett and Marjorie Rhodes. This comfortable comedy is about unconsummated marriage of a pair of newly-weds forced to share a house with the folks.

Persona is an example of director Ingmar Bergman at his best, a very complex exploration of art, reality and communication in which Liv Ullmann and Bibi Andersson merge into a single woman.

And there were dozens and dozens of others, the best of which included *Harper, Tokyo Drifter, The Blue Max, Closely Observed Trains, The Rise to Power of Louis XIV, Hawks and Sparrows, The Face of Another, The Big TNT Show, The Trap, Seconds, Django* and *Andrei Rublev.*

THEATRE

A number of long-runners were going, such as *The Mousetrap*, which was at The Ambassadors Theatre until it was moved to St Martin's in 1974. But the year saw a number of new shows hit London's West End.

At the Royal Court in Sloane Square, where John Osborne's *Look Back in Anger* had caused a stir in 1956 and where *Chips with Everything* had been such a big hit in 1962, there was a new play, *The Knack*, Ann Jellicoe's play which was also a film starring Michael Crawford and Ray Brooks.

And at the same place, in May, came *Their Very Own and Golden City*, written by Arnold Wesker and starring a very young Ian McKellen. There was also a memorable *Macbeth* here that year, starring Alec Guinness, with Gordon Jackson, later better known for his television roles in *Upstairs, Downstairs* and *The Professionals*, as Banquo.

At the Palladium in Argyll Street, famous for its productions of *The King and I* and *Joseph and the Amazing Technicolor Dreamcoat*, there came *London Laughs*, starring Thora Hird, Freddie Frinton and Jimmy Tarbuck, with the singer Anita Harris and Russ Conway on the piano. That great farceur, Brian Rix, was at The Whitehall regularly in the 1950s and 1960s. And this year it was with *Come Spy With Me*, with Barbara Windsor.

At The Globe in Shaftesbury Avenue, now known as the Gielgud Theatre, where more recently Kathleen Turner starred in *The Graduate*, the long-running *There's a Girl in My Soup* opened, with Donald Sinden and John Pertwee. And at St Martin's Lane there was *The Killing of Sister George*.

The Royal Shakespeare Company, based at The Aldwych at the time, made way for a more contemporary offering, *US*, which means not you and me but the United States. Directed by Peter Brook and starring Glenda Jackson, it was an anti-war offering at a time when Vietnam was a hot issue on both sides of the Atlantic.

Spike Milligan, famous for his Goon scripts, starred in *The Sitting Room* at The Mermaid.

In panto season, *Peter Pan* came to The Escala, starring Julia Lockwood, with Ron Moody. Cliff Richard played Buttons at The Palladium, and he was supported by The Shadows. And at The Comedy Theatre, that wonderful little home of entertainment in Panton Street, with its great display of photographs, playbills and programmes, Richard Goolden starred in *Toad of Toad Hall*.

BIRTHS IN 1966

20 February	Cindy Crawford, supermodel
24 February	Billy Zane, American actor
31 March	Roger Black, British athlete
28 April	John Daly, American golfer and winner of two Majors
29 April	Phil Tufnell, cricketer
10 May	Jonathan Edwards, triple-jump Olympic gold medallist
16 May	Janet Jackson, singer
24 May	Eric Cantona, former Manchester United and France footballer
26 May	Helena Bonham-Carter, English actress
30 June	Mike Tyson, former heavyweight boxing champion
14 August	Halle Berry, actress
21 September	Kiefer Sutherland, actor

DEATHS IN 1966

1 February — Buster Keaton, American actor and film director. One of the great silent film actors, Keaton made only ten feature films in the Twenties but was regarded as a greater comic actor than Charlie Chaplin.

9 February — Sophie Tucker, American music-hall singer

2 April — C.S. Forester, author of the Hornblower books

Buster Keaton – a giant of the silent screen.
(John Kobal Foundation/Getty Images)

10 April

Evelyn Waugh, author. Waugh was one of the great English novelists and wrote classics such as *Brideshead Revisited*,

Scoop and *A Handful of Dust*. Towards the end of his life he lived the life of a Catholic squire in Somerset and renounced twentieth-century innovations, refusing to have a television or radio in his house. He even used an ear trumpet.

Celebrated author Evelyn Waugh lived the life of a Somerset squire before his death in 1966. *(Kurt Hutton/Getty Images)*

23 July

Montgomery Clift, American actor. A Hollywood star of the Fifties, Clift was a bisexual who had affairs with Elizabeth

Taylor and Marilyn Monroe. He survived a horrific car crash in 1956 which badly disfigured his face.

Hollywood legend Montgomery Clift, who died in July, with one of his co-stars Elizabeth Taylor. *(Getty Images)*

4 August

Lenny Bruce, American comedian

18 October

Elizabeth Arden, cosmetics entrepreneur

15 December

Walt Disney. The creator of cartoon characters such as Mickey Mouse, Donald Duck and Pluto, Disney became a worldwide entertainment phenomenon. His first full-length feature film was *Snow White and the Seven Dwarfs*, which was made in 1937.

Walt Disney. *(Getty Images)*

KEY DATES IN BRITAIN IN 1966

JANUARY

4 4,000 people attend a memorial service in Westminster Abbey for the broadcaster Richard Dimbleby.

7 The government announces a joint relief effort with Australia and Canada for drought-stricken Rhodesia.

13 The Rhodesian government expels three Labour MPs on a fact-finding mission.

17 Leading British bakers put a penny on the price of a standard loaf which rises to 1s 3½d (about 7 pence).

29 A bill permitting the first roadside random breath tests is published in Parliament, setting the legal limit at 80mg of alcohol per 100cl of blood. A driver in a stationary vehicle would be exempt provided that he could prove he was intending to wait before driving.

31 The Board of Trade bans nearly all trade between London and Rhodesia in protest at Unilateral Declaration of Independence (UDI).

Reveille, a weekly compendium of short stories, crosswords and competitions, had a circulation of 1,170,986 in 1966, an increase of 42,000 on the previous year. Among its contributors in 1966 were P.G. Wodehouse. The magazine's popularity was on the wane by the end of the decade, however, and it closed in 1973.

FEBRUARY

3 The Companies Bill, which made it law for firms to reveal donations to political parties, is published.

9 The government announces plans for a fast-breeder nuclear reactor at Dounreay, in Scotland.

10 Watneys put up the price of a pint of beer to 1s 8d (about 9 pence).

19 Christopher Mayhew resigns as Navy Minister over 'dangerously mistaken' defence policies.

27 Shell Oil UK reports that it has struck oil in both Muscat and Oman.

Scientists at the National Coal Board claimed they had invented the world's first 'hot paint' which gave off instant central heating when applied to walls.

MARCH

1   Chancellor of the Exchequer James Callaghan confirms that Britain will switch to decimal currency in 1971.

3   The BBC announces plans to broadcast in colour in 1967.

Britain's first coloured policeman was sworn into the Coventry force in March. PC Mohamed Yusuf Daar, 23, nearly doubled his earnings after leaving his factory job. PC Daar, who was born in Nairobi and spoke six languages, was suitably overwhelmed: 'This is a wonderful day for me,' he said.

In a reorganisation of Britain's policing announced in May, Home Secretary Roy Jenkins confirmed that the number of forces would be slashed by 68 from 117 to 49.

5   A British Boeing 707 crashes into Mount Fuji; 130 passengers die.

7   The government announces plans to abolish National Assistance and replace it with a new Ministry of Social Security.

15 The Royal Air Force is granted a base from Madagascar from which to patrol the African coast for sanctions-busters.

On 8 March, Ronnie Kray shot rival gangster George Cornell in the Blind Beggar pub, East London. By then Ronnie, his twin Reggie and their elder brother Charlie had such a grip on the London underworld that police could not find a single witness to the fatal shooting. Ronnie was eventually jailed for life for the murder of Cornell in 1969. He died of a heart attack in Broadmoor Hospital in 1995.

The infamous Kray twins, Ronnie and Reggie, controlled London's criminal underworld. (Copyright © popperfoto.com)

20 The World Cup trophy goes missing from an exhibition in London's Westminster
    Central Hall. It is found a few days later by a dog, Pickles, wrapped in
    newspaper in a London garden.

**The Exchange Telegraph (Extel) news agency, which had served Fleet
Street for sixty years, flashed its last news message in 1966 although
its sports service continued for another two decades. Among its
scoops was news of the first nuclear bombs to be exploded by Britain.**

APRIL

1   The British Airports Authority, which controls all major airports in the UK, is
    formed.
5   Shell Oil strikes oil off the coast at Great Yarmouth, describing the find as one of
    'considerable importance'.
8   Government figures show the number of illegitimate births in England and Wales
    has nearly doubled between 1956 and 1966.
14 The Sussex Downs are designated an Area of Outstanding Natural Beauty.

**In April, the first regular cross-Channel hovercraft service began. It
would continue until 2000, when the Channel Tunnel was finally
opened.**

19 Ted Heath reshuffles the shadow cabinet in the wake of the Conservatives'
    election defeat, sacking Selwyn Lloyd and Ernest Marples.
21 The State Opening of Parliament is televised for the first time.
25 Lord Cromer is succeeded by Leslie O'Brien as Governor of the Bank of England.
30 Hoverlloyd begins the first scheduled cross-Channel hovercraft service between
    Ramsgate and Calais.

**One of the biggest criminal trials of the decade ended in May when
the notorious Moors Murderers, Ian Brady, 28, and 23-year-old
Myra Hindley, were jailed. Together, the pair were responsible for the
brutal murders of five schoolchildren – Pauline Reade, John Kilbride,
Keith Bennett, Lesley Ann Downey and Edward Evans – between
1963 and 1965. All five were buried on Saddleworth Moor, near
Oldham, although Keith's body has never been found. Hindley was
found guilty of the Evans and Downey murders but not the Kilbride
murder. Brady was arrested immediately after the murder of Edward
Evans when the victim's 18-year-old brother-in-law went to the
police after Brady and Hindley had invited him to become involved
with the killing.**

At Chester Crown Court, Brady was given three concurrent terms of life imprisonment, the death penalty having been abolished in 1965. Hindley was found guilty of murdering Lesley and Edward and given two life sentences, plus seven years for being an accessory to Brady in the murder of John.

Brady, who earlier in his life had been known as 'The Undertaker' and 'Dracula', was an illegitimate product of Glasgow's notorious Gorbals estate. Born in 1938, he made his first court appearance at the age of 13 on charges of housebreaking. Two years later he went to live with his mother in Manchester and soon slipped back into crime. Brady and Hindley developed their mutual admiration of Hitler and Nazism after meeting in 1961. Hindley carried with her a photograph of the notorious 'Beast of Belsen', Irma Grese.

Mr Justice Fenton Atkinson told the court after handing down the sentences: 'It should be said that these matters were only brought to light by police investigation of the utmost skill.'

Brady has been force-fed since 1999 after going on hunger strike at the secure Ashworth Psychiatric Hospital on Merseyside. Hindley died of a heart attack in 2002.

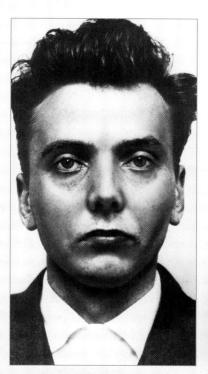

Moors Murderers Ian Brady and Myra Hindley. *(Copyright © Popperfoto)*

MAY

4 The government announces pay rises for doctors and dentists working in the NHS of between 10 and 35 per cent. Doctors can now expect to earn around £4,000 a year.

17 Transport minister Barbara Castle confirms that the new 70mph speed limit will remain in force at least until 1967.
Former world middleweight boxing champion Randolph Turpin is found dead in his flat in Leamington Spa, Warwickshire.

18 Home secretary Roy Jenkins confirms that the number of police forces in England and Wales will be slashed by 68.

Timothy John Evans, who had been hanged sixteen years earlier for the murder of his young daughter, was granted a posthumous free pardon, unprecedented in British legal history, by the Queen in October.

Evans, who was born in Wales, moved to London in 1948 with his wife Beryl. Their daughter Geraldine was born a year later. In 1949 Mrs Evans became pregnant again. Their neighbour, the infamous mass murderer John Christie, offered to get her an abortion, which was illegal at the time.

Evans came home in November 1949 to find his wife dead. Christie threatened to implicate Evans unless he co-operated. Evans confessed after the bodies of his wife and child were found at 10 Rillington Place. Christie gave evidence against him at his murder trial and although Evans attempted to implicate Christie, he was

convicted and hanged after an appeal was dismissed. It was eventually discovered that Christie, a mass murderer who was hanged in 1953 for the murder of his wife, had killed Beryl and Geraldine Evans. A high-profile campaign by journalist Ludovic Kennedy and barrister Michael Eddowes fought to clear Evans and he was eventually granted a pardon. The outcry over the case and the subsequent miscarriage of justice eventually led to the abolition of the death penalty in Britain.

John Christie, guilty of the murders for which Timothy Evans was hanged. *(Getty Images)*

A high-profile campaign led by the journalist Ludovic Kennedy brought a posthumous free pardon for Timothy Evans. *(Harry Dempster/Express/Getty Images)*

Timothy Evans, hanged for murders he did not commit. *(Keystone/Getty Images)*

JUNE

1 UK Phillips Petroleum claim to have made the richest North Sea gas strike yet.

6 The BBC broadcasts the first episode of *Till Death Us Do Part*. Two days later the Conservative Party asks for a copy of the script, claiming that its leader, Ted Heath, had been described as a 'grammar school twit'.

11 Mary Quant and Peter Sellers receive OBEs at Buckingham Palace.

In June, the AA announced that its annual subscription would go up the following January from two to three guineas – the first rise since 1905, when the Automobile Association was founded. The rise was announced after the AA reported a £68,000 profit in 1964 had turned into a £188,000 deficit in 1965. The organisation's treasurer, Lord Fraser of Allander, said the increase was unavoidable because of the rising cost of maintaining the fleet of recovery vehicles.

20 James White is sentenced to twenty years' imprisonment for his part in the Great Train Robbery.

28 Prime Minister Harold Wilson claims that Communists are using the seamen's strike to effect a power struggle in the National Union of Seamen.

Budget airlines are a relatively new phenomenon. But Freddie Laker launched his low-cost airline, Laker Airways, in 1966, operating cheap flights to popular summer and winter destinations in Europe before launching his transatlantic service in 1973. It lasted nine years before the airline went bust in 1982.

His first fleet were three One-Eleven 75-seaters purchased from BAC for £4 million. Laker, a self-made millionaire, who started in the business in 1946 with his £40 RAF gratuity, invested £211,000 of his own money in the project. His wife, Joan, was the only other director and the fleet was painted in his racing colours of red, black and white. He promised that no one would have to fly a propellor-driven aircraft after 1968.

After the company went bust, the pioneer of the budget airline retired to the Bahamas. He died in February 2006.

JULY

3 Frank Cousins resigns as Minister of Technology and is replaced by Anthony Wedgwood Benn. The former union leader opposed Harold Wilson's proposed pay restraint legislation.

Pioneer of the skies. Freddie Laker introduced low-cost air travel. *(Central Press/Getty Images)*

There are thirty-one arrests at an anti-Vietnam War demonstration in London's Grosvenor Square.

4   The government publishes the Prices and Incomes Bill.

11   BMC and Jaguar announce they are to merge to become British Motor Holdings.

14   The bank rate is raised 1 per cent to 7 per cent.

21   Gywnfor Evans becomes the first Welsh Nationalist MP in Parliament after he wins the Carmarthen by-election.

27   The Trades Union Congress backs Harold Wilson's wages freeze which was designed to curb rampant inflation.

One of the biggest manhunts in British criminal history began after three unarmed policemen were shot in west London on 12 August 1966. Before then, police killing in Britain was almost unheard of.

Detective Sergeant Christopher Head, aged 30, Detective Constable David Wombwell, 25, and 41-year-old Constable Geoffrey Fox had just finished collecting exhibits from Marylebone Magistrates Court when they flagged down a Standard Vanguard Estate which was making a lot of noise on a street close to Wormwood Scrubs Prison in west London. Wombwell and Head went to investigate the car and its three occupants but moments later Wombwell lay dead on the pavement, killed by a single bullet to the forehead from a 9mm Luger pistol fired by the front-seat passenger, Harry Maurice Roberts.

As Sgt Head tried to escape to the patrol car, Roberts stepped out of the Vanguard and shot him in the back of the head. PC Fox was killed by three shots from a .38 Colt service revolver fired by John Duddy, a passenger in the back of the Vanguard.

The killers snatched PC Wombwell's notebook and headed in the direction of Hammersmith before dumping the car in south London. There were several witnesses to the murders, which took place shortly after 3 p.m., including several schoolchildren who thought the gunshots they heard were a crew filming a television programme. One eye-witness noted the car's registration plates because he thought there had been a jailbreak from Wormwood Scrubs. Within hours John Witney, the owner and driver of the car, had been arrested in London.

Six days after the shootings Duddy was picked up in Glasgow but finding Roberts took much longer. The hunt for the killer became something of a national obsession. Police logged over 6,000 reported sightings while for the first time since 1954 crime figures in the capital fell as numerous raids brought the criminal underworld to a standstill. More than £5,000 was raised for the families of the three policemen and there were over 700 mourners, many from the general public, at a memorial service five weeks later.

The manhunt for Roberts spread far and wide. One tip-off led to 2,000 officers searching Sadler's Wells theatre while a production of Offenbach's opera *Bluebeard* was taking place. Eventually, on 18 November – three months after the murders – Roberts was apprehended.

His hideout in Thorley Wood near Bishops Stortford, Essex, had been discovered by a gypsy, but it wasn't until the following day that two police sergeants, Peter Smith and Oswald Thorne, found Roberts in a disused barn full of hay bales.

'Please don't shoot,' Roberts told them. 'You won't get any trouble from me, I've had enough.'

Roberts' carefully constructed hideout, made from a tarpaulin covered with used fertiliser bags painted green and black, was later auctioned and the proceeds given to a police fund.

The trial of the other two accused, Witney and Duddy, had already begun and was only into its second day when Roberts was picked up. It had to be adjourned, but on 12 December all three received life sentences. Summing up, Judge Glyn Jones called it 'the most heinous crime to have been committed in this country for a generation or more'.

Six years later Roberts made an audacious bid to tunnel through the 3ft-wide wall of Parkhurst maximum security prison on the Isle of Wight before his escape bid was foiled.

The murder of three policemen in Shepherd's Bush in August shocked the country. (Douglas Miller/Keystone/Getty Images)

METROPOLITAN POLICE

£1,000 REWARD
MURDER

A reward or rewards up to a total of £1,000 will be paid for information leading to the arrest of HARRY MAURICE ROBERTS, b. Wanstead, Essex, on 21-7-36, 5ft. 10in., photo. above, wanted for questioning in connection with the murder of three police officers on the 12th August, 1966, at Braybrook Street, Shepherds Bush.

Information to be given to New Scotland Yard, S.W.1, or at any police station.

The amount of any payment will be in the discretion of the Commissioner of Police for the Metropolis.

J. SIMPSON,
Commissioner of Police.

Wanted Man. The murder of three policemen in West London sparked a huge manhunt for Harry Roberts. *(Copyright © popperfoto.com)*

AUGUST

4   The Kray twins are taken in for questioning over the murder of Jack Cornell in the Blind Beggar pub.

10   George Brown succeeds Michael Stewart as Foreign Secretary.

22   Plans are announced for a 385ft skyscraper with thirty-four floors in London's West End, called Centre Point.

A West Indian man who was refused a job at Euston Station in August was finally given employment there after managers overturned a ban on black workers.

Two months earlier Asquith Xavier, a train guard from Dominica, was refused a transfer from Marylebone Station to Euston because of his colour. The new job would have meant a pay rise of around £10 a week for Mr Xavier who had worked as a porter for British Rail for ten years. He was told of his rejection and the reason for it in a letter from Euston's local staff committee whose members belonged to the National Union of Railwaymen.

23   The Cotswolds are designated an Area of Outstanding Natural Beauty.
31   A British airliner crashes in Yugoslavia, killing ninety-two passengers and crew.

Ronald 'Buster' Edwards, one of the thirteen Great Train Robbers, gave himself up to police in September. Edwards had been on the run in Mexico for three years since the heist in 1963 when £2.3 million – the equivalent of £40 million today – was stolen from a mail train in Buckinghamshire. Edwards eventually received a life sentence and ran a flower stall in London after his release. He committed suicide in 1994, aged 62.

Great Train Robber Buster Edwards gave himself up after three years on the run. *(Leonard Burt/Central Press/Getty Images)*

SEPTEMBER

10   The West End's longest-running musical, *Oliver!* ends its run of six years, three months.
15   The Queen Mother launches Britain's first nuclear submarine, HMS *Resolution*, at Barrow-in-Furness.
20   The Hawker-Siddeley Harrier, the world's first vertical take-off and landing aircraft, is unveiled at the Farnborough Air Show.

The Queen opened the Severn Bridge in September. More than a mile long, the construction was in fact two bridges. The larger one spanned the Severn Estuary, the smaller bridge crossed the River Wye.

27 Ten weeks after its merger with Jaguar, car giant BMC announces 7,000 lay-offs and plans a further 11,000 redundancies for later in the year.

30 Canadian press baron Lord Thomson buys *The Times*.

Britain's first credit card was introduced by Barclaycard.

OCTOBER

4   The government introduces a prices and wages freeze under the new Prices and Incomes Act.

11 Car manufacturer Jensen unveils its two new models – the Interceptor and the FF – in London.
    The Post Office confirms that every home and business address in Britain is to have its own postcode with effect from 5 November. Croydon (CR) becomes the first area to be given a postcode.

27 Prime Minister Harold Wilson announces he will make no more recommendations for honours for political service.

29 The British Army drops its colour bar.

31 Production of Austin and Morris cars is brought to a halt by strike action against the company's redundancy plans for 11,000 of its workers, designed to bring BMC back into profitability.

The General Post Office issued its first set of Christmas stamps in 1966. The stamps were designed by children after the GPO ran a nationwide competition.

NOVEMBER

7   The government admits its concern at the alarming 'brain drain' of British scientists and engineers to the United States which has increased by 22 per cent in the past four years. Doctors are also believed to be emigrating in particularly large numbers.

9   Jack Lynch, a former All-Ireland footballer from Cork, is named as the new Irish Prime Minister. Lynch pledges to continue to build relations between the south and north of Ireland.

11 The unofficial stoppage which halted car production at BMC is called off.

13 Supporters of Rhodesian Prime Minister Ian Smith stage a peaceful Remembrance Sunday demonstration outside Downing Street.

23 BP confirms that it has struck its best gas-producing area yet in the North Sea, about forty miles off the Humber estuary.

24 Unemployment in Britain rises by nearly 100,000 in the previous month, to 531,585.

25 Warren Mitchell, star of BBC's new comedy *Till Death Us Do Part*, is named best TV comedy actor of 1966.

30 In a speech in London, Harold Wilson urges Europe to build up its economy to avoid US economic domination.

DECEMBER

2 Harold Wilson holds talks with Ian Smith on board *HMS Tiger* in the Mediterranean about the continuing crisis in Rhodesia. Wilson calls for Smith to repudiate UDI, bring at least two black Africans into his cabinet and surrender control of his armed forces. Four days later Smith emerges from a ten-hour cabinet meeting to reject the proposals, insisting: 'The fight goes on.'
Wilson asks the United Nations to impose trade sanctions on Rhodesia.

5 Frank Cousins resigns as Labour MP for Nuneaton to concentrate on his career in the trade union movement.

12 The Gas Council confirms another successful gas strike in the North Sea.

22 Rhodesia resigns from the Commonwealth.

BIBLIOGRAPHY

The following books were consulted, in addition to copies of *The Times*, *Sun*, *Daily Express*, *Radio Times*, *New Musical Express* and *Western Mail*.

Astaire, J. *Encounters*, Robson Books, 1999
Banks, G. *Banksy*, Penguin Books, 2002
Butler, D. and King, A. *The British General Election of 1966*, Macmillan, 1966
Campbell, T. and Potter, D. *Jock Stein: The Celtic Years*, Mainstream Publishing, 1998
Charlton, J. *My Autobiography*, Corgi Books, 1998
Evans, J. *The Penguin TV Companion*, Penguin Books, 2003
Glanville, B. *History of the World Cup*, Faber & Faber, 1973
Hauser, T. *Muhammad Ali – His Life and Times*, Pan, 1991
James, B. *England v Scotland*, Pelham Press, 1969
Joyce, P. *UK General Elections 1832–2000*, Methuen, 2004
Kilburn, M. *London's Theatres*, New Holland Publishers, 2002
Lanning, J. *Great Disasters*, Treasure Press, 1976
Larkin, C. *Who's Who of Sixties Music*, Guinness Publishing, 1992
Laybourn, K. *A Century of Labour*, Sutton Publishing, 2000
Lee, L. *I Can't Stay Long*, André Deutsch, 1967
McKinstry, L. *Jack and Bobby: A Story of Brothers in Conflict*, Partridge Press, 2003
McLean, I. and Johnes, M. *Aberfan: Government and Disasters*, Welsh Academic Press, 2000
The Macmillan International Film Encyclopedia, Macmillan
Norman, P. *Shout! The Beatles Story*, Pan, 1981
Peel, C. *Cricketing Falstaff*, André Deutsch, 1998
Radio Times Film Guide, BBC, 1993
Ross, G. (ed) *Playfair Cricket Annual 1967*, Playfair, 1967
Stiles, N. *After the Ball*, Hodder & Stoughton, 2003
Thomson, D. *The New Biographical Dictionary of Film*, Alfred A.Knopf, 2004
Time Out Film Guide 2005, Time Out Group, 2004
Ward, A. *Soccer's Strangest Matches*, Robson Books, 1989
Wisden Cricketer's Almanac 1967, John Wisden, 1967

INDEX